THE BOSTON MASSACRE
An Episode of Dissent and Violence

The BOSTON MASSACRE

❦

An Episode of Dissent and Violence

BY HARRY HANSEN

200TH ANNIVERSARY EDITION

*Illustrated with Photographs
by Samuel Chamberlain*

HASTINGS HOUSE *Publishers* New York 10016

Published simultaneously in Canada by
Saunders, of Toronto, Ltd. Don Mills, Ontario
SBN: 8038-0724-4

Library of Congress Catalog Card Number: 73-90281
Printed in the United States of America

CONTENTS

ILLUSTRATIONS

Two Hundred Years Ago— and Today

EXACTLY two hundred years ago the American colonies entered the decisive phase of their disagreement with the taxing policies of Great Britain, which led to the Revolution and subsequent independence. After trying by every legal device to retain the right to tax themselves for internal use, the colonists became convinced that the British Government would continue to tax them for revenue to pay its expenses in peace and war, and would use force to collect that tax. The event that made many undecided colonists lean toward united action was the Boston Massacre of March 5, 1770.

On that night a squad of British foot soldiers, called out to protect a sentry from a Boston mob, fired on the civilians, killing four, fatally wounding a fifth, and injuring six others. The soldiers had been outrageously baited, but belonged to a regiment that for months had jostled and threatened the townsmen, who resented its presence as an unwarranted intrusion of the military into a community that was at peace.

It was not a massacre in the sense that large numbers were killed, but the word was being used quite freely whenever Indians raided settlements, and was applied immediately to this occurrence. John Adams, who defended the soldiers in court, admitted they had provocation, but added: "This, however, is no reason why the town should not call the action of that night a massacre." It has been called "the first battle of the American Revolution" by some, but that moves the true event ahead by five years. Daniel Webster, carried away by patriotic emotion, announced: "From that moment we may date the severance from the British Empire," which is another exaggeration. We can, however, confidently call it a milestone along the march of the American colonies to the supreme moment of July 4, 1776. It showed in high relief the grievous hurt done British-American relations by the quartering of troops in a colonial town to enforce unwanted laws. That soldiers actually would fire on and kill dissenting Americans was not believed possible until it actually took place. It did not matter that the troops had been subjected to excessive provocation; the enormity was that they used their guns at all. This converted many to the belief that should the colonies reject new duties forced upon them, the troops would shoot again.

The relation of dissent to violence, and the attitude taken by both sides to the quarrel after March 5, 1770, is a subject of engrossing interest to Americans today. Judgment on any event in human experience is never closed. Every generation makes a new assessment of the past, in the light of its own amplified knowledge, or from its own point of view. The culmination of a series of irritants in harassment is a familiar spectacle, and the lessons that can be drawn from it are as pertinent today as they were in the eighteenth century. The Boston Massacre, on a police record, would be a street brawl of a few hours' duration. But its political influence was far-reaching; its part in stiffening resistance to arbitrary rule a vital one.

And today there are new measuring sticks. As of this hour, there is the relation of mob behavior to the principles of dissent. There is the example of restraint in punishing individuals, in order to safeguard the welfare of a whole society. And finally there is the new emphasis on the sacrifice of one of the mob—Crispus Attucks, half Negro, half Indian—to show the participation of a member of the ethnic minority in the beginnings of this nation.

I The Military Occupation

1

The British Army in Boston

In March, 1770, the crucial month of this chronicle, Boston was an occupied town. It had been compelled to accept the presence of two regiments of British regulars, the 14th West Yorkshire Fuseliers, and the 29th Worcestershire, which had arrived from Halifax in September, 1768. For eighteen months they had treated the inhabitants with insolence, posted sentries in front of public offices, engaged in street fights with the town boys, and used the Boston Common for flogging unruly soldiers and exercising troops.

The regiments had been ordered to Boston to protect the men who collected customs duties for the owner of Boston, the King of England. The Commissioners of Customs, who acquired their jobs in Britain and drew their pay from what they collected in America, were so intimidated by the resistance they met in Boston that they demanded military protection. The Governor of the Province, Francis Bernard, was willing to ask for troops, but could not get the assent of the Council; however, Lord Hillsborough, Secretary of State for the Colonies, had advised General Thomas Gage, commander in chief of the British Army in America, of his duty to protect the royal services, and Bernard agreed. Thereupon two regiments were ordered to Boston from Halifax, and two more alerted in Ireland.

The troops arrived in eight warships and auxiliary vessels and landed on the Long Wharf, whence they marched in full military array with fixed bayonets as if investing a hostile town. In addition to the two regiments there were a detachment of the 59th Regiment and a train of artillery with two cannon, in all about 700 men. To the further exasperation of the townspeople they landed on the morning of Sunday, September 28.

The scene was recorded for posterity by Paul Revere in an engraving that also explains: "They marched with insolent parade, drums beating, fifes playing, and colors flying, up King Street. Each soldier having received sixteen rounds of powder and ball." The cartouche says: "To the Earl of Hillsborough . . . this view of the only well-planned expedition formed for supporting ye dignity of Britain in chastising the insolence of America, is humbly dedicated."

General Gage, whose headquarters were located in New York, had explained to Governor Bernard the instructions he had given Lieut. Colonel William Dalrymple, who was to command in Boston. He was to strengthen the hands of the government in the Province of Massachusetts, enforce obedience to the laws, protect, support, and give legal assistance to the civil magistrates in the preservation of peace, and to the revenue officers in the execution of the laws of trade and revenue. "The use that shall be made of the troops to effect these purposes," wrote Gage, "I am to leave to the direction and management of the civil power."

To the people of Boston the coming of the troops was outrageous. They had been fighting for years against infringement by Britain of their right to tax themselves, so that they regarded the troops as insufferable coercion. When Governor Bernard asked the town to provide quarters, the leading townsmen refused, recommending the use of the barracks at Castle William, on an island three miles off shore. Bernard retorted that these were wanted for regiments from Ireland. The troops finally were given temporary quarters in Faneuil Hall and several other public buildings and raised tents on the Common before obtaining the use of warehouses.

Hours before the troops landed the patriots who were defending the rights of the Province had just completed another round of arguments with Governor Bernard. The town meeting, with Samuel Adams, John Adams, Thomas Cushing, John Hancock, James Otis, Jr., and other liberals leading, had asked the Governor to call a meeting of the General Court, the official name for the Assembly, and when he refused they summoned each town in the Province to name a delegate to a convention in Boston, for the ostensible purpose of discussing the "prevailing apprehension of war with France." All except one of the sixty-six towns responded; the convention voted an appeal to the King for a redress of grievances, and protested that they were loyal and not rebellious. All the grievances of the Province were spelled out, and letters were sent to the friends of Massachusetts in Britain describing the situation. Governor Bernard denied the right of the people to assemble peacefully and threatened the leaders with punishment if they persisted. He addressed a formal message to "Gentlemen assembled at Faneuil Hall under the name of a committee or convention," in which he said: "As I have lately received from his majesty strict orders to support his constitutional authority within this government, I cannot sit still and see such a notorious violation of it as calling an assembly of people by private persons only. For a meeting of the deputies of the towns is an assembly of the representatives of the people to all intents and purposes, and it is not the calling it a committee or convention that will alter the nature of the thing. I am willing to believe that the gentlemen who so hastily issued the summons for this meeting were not aware of the high nature of the offense they were committing . . ."

He admonished them to break up the assembly and separate before doing any business. "If you pay no regard to this admonition, I must, as Governor, assert the prerogative of the Crown in a more public manner. For assure yourselves (I speak from instruction) the King is determined to maintain his entire sovereignty over this Province, and whoever shall persist in usurping any of the rights of it will repent of his rashness."

The convention met for four days, advised peaceful protests against violations of the rights of the Province, expressed continued loyalty to the King, and adjourned one day before the British troops arrived from Halifax. Other colonies followed the example of Massachusetts in holding interstate meetings and the movement became an important channel for communications and tactics. Instead of following up his warnings, Bernard left for England next spring and was created Baronet of Nettleham. In a letter to the *Boston Gazette* signed "A Tory" Samuel

Adams ironically congratulated Bernard on his exalted honor.

The entry of the troops was the direct result of Boston's defiance of the Commissioners of Customs. The incident that brought public resentment against the tax collectors to a head came about with the arrival of John Hancock's sloop, *Liberty*, on June 10, 1768, with a cargo of Madeira wine. This was one of the articles on which duties had been raised lately. As always the tideman, Kirke, went aboard at 9 P.M. to confer with the captain in his cabin about the cargo. The captain and his men confined Kirke to the cabin, while others landed the wine without entering it for duty and stowed it in Hancock's warehouse. Next day the customs office ordered the sloop seized, and the controller, Hallowell, removed the sloop from the dock to a place close beside the British warship *Romney*, then standing in the harbor. The presence of the *Romney* for no good reason had disturbed the Boston public for some time. The Sons of Liberty now held a protest meeting in Faneuil Hall and demanded that Governor Bernard remove the warship. The crowd became a mob, which seized a boat used by the commissioners, dragged it to the Common, and there burned it. Hallowell, who had had his house ransacked during the Stamp Act riot, and feared more trouble from the mob, now fled with his fellow commissioners to Castle William in the harbor.

There was little doubt that the royal governor needed support, and that the revenue officers needed protection. Governor Bernard had put in nearly nine years trying to enforce the laws and proclamations issued by Parliament in London, and he had met with opposition and sometimes open defiance from the Assembly, or lower house, of the General Court of Massachusetts, which was elected by the people, and at times even from the Council, or upper body, which had members chosen from the House, whose election he could approve or veto. He had asked for troops when the rioting over the Stamp Act was at its peak, but had been overruled. His only powers lay in obstruction; he could keep the Assembly from meeting, or move it to a place outside of Boston, and he could dominate the acts of royal officials, but otherwise, as he admitted, the people possessed the power and he was helpless. Now, even with the military at hand, he found his methods of enforcement futile. He held out less than a year after the troops arrived; in 1769 he turned his office over to the Lieutenant Governor, Thomas Hutchinson, and on the date with which we are chiefly concerned, March 5, 1770, Hutchinson was Acting Governor of the Province of Massachusetts.

There was no pardoning the rampaging behavior of the street mobs. To what extent they understood the points of law raised by leaders of the patriots is problematical, but that they were ready at all times to demonstrate in favor of liberty and against the royal authority is evident. The leaders—Samuel Adams, John Adams, William Cooper, Thomas Cushing, John Hancock, James Otis, Joseph Warren, James Warren, numerous others—though firm in their adherence to Great Britain, for years had reiterated the right of the colonies to levy internal taxes and denied this right to Parliament because the colonies were not represented there. While they fought with arguments, resolutions, and leaflets within the bounds of legality, the more active Sons of Liberty engaged in direct action. At any time they were ready to demonstrate in the streets and stage all sorts of noisy affairs, such as ridiculing uncooperative merchants on placards and signboards, hanging effigies of British officials responsible for inequitable taxes, and treating collectors of customs to jeers and threats. Once these groups were on the march they were joined by bands of toughs who left off fighting one another to riot in the name of liberty. They ransacked houses, destroyed gardens, damaged records and tossed books and silver plate out of windows. Royal officials admitted privately to London that they were helpless; the democratic element dominated the town meetings and the Assembly, and conservative measures could not get a hearing.

John Adams, a lawyer on horseback, returned from a circuit-riding trip to county courts to find Boston full of redcoats. He set down that "their very appearance in Boston was a strong proof to me that the determination of Great Britain to subjugate us was too deep and inveterate ever to be altered by us." Other patriots, jealous of the privileges and rights written into the charters and patents in force since the seventeenth century, had been apprehensive ever since the end of the French and Indian War—called the Seven Years' War in Britain. The British had left a substantial army in America to accomplish the transition from French to British rule in Canada, and to police the huge area reaching from the Appalachians to the Mississippi River, part of which had been known as New France. The actual ruler of this domain was General Gage, who reviewed military decisions reached as far apart as Montreal, Detroit, and Fort de Chartres.

And now General Gage had planted the military power in Boston. Every day the townsmen were made aware of the soldiers. During the fall and winter of 1768 a regiment was exercised daily in Brattle Square, in front of the house of John Adams, who recalled: "The spirit-stirring drum, and the ear-piercing fife, aroused me and my family early enough every morning, and the indigestion they excited, though somewhat soothed, was not allayed by the sweet songs, violins and flutes of the serenading Sons of Liberty under my windows in the evening."

Benjamin Franklin commented in his temperate way that keeping a standing army in America without consent of the Assemblies was not "agreeable to the Constitution." There was to be a long debate about that.

2

Royalist and Democrat

THOMAS HUTCHINSON, Lieutenant Governor and Acting
Governor in 1770, was the leader of the royal faction and a
man of considerable ability. Boston born and bred, 59 years
old, he had his roots in American soil as firmly as any of
the Sons of Liberty, yet his whole career, with few excep-
tions, had been devoted to defending the British prerogatives. His experiences at the hands of the patriots had made
him apprehensive and led him to approve the call for
troops, though it did not emanate from him. The constant
opposition to laws passed by Parliament had worn him
down, and about this time he wrote General Gage: "In
matters of dispute between the King and the colonies government is at an end and in the hands of the people."

The son of a wealthy merchant, Hutchinson had attended Harvard College, engaged briefly in business, then
studied English constitutional law and embraced a public
career. He became so efficient in acquiring public offices for
himself and his kin that he alienated the public. At first he

was elected to the Assembly as Representative with popular support, and served ten years, three of them as Speaker. He became a judge of probate in Suffolk County and a member of the Council, the upper legislative house, and was already Lieutenant Governor when Governor Bernard, disregarding popular pressure, named him Chief Justice in 1760. He continued to hold both offices and push his kin into others. He approved the Writs of Assistance, which gave customs men blanket rights of search and seizure, but did not approve the Stamp Act.

His name would shine with special luster in American history if, like another rich man, John Hancock, he had recognized and supported the democratic trend, but he had no confidence in ability of the people to govern. This was all the more lamentable because behind him towers the figure of his rebellious ancestress, the unyielding Anne Hutchinson, who 130 years before had defied the overbearing theocracy of Massachusetts Bay Colony and suffered banishment. Anne and her husband, William Hutchinson, had emigrated from Lincolnshire in 1634, and her whole career had been a battle against the attempts of the Puritan ministry to regulate the relations of the individual to his God. Hutchinson described her defiance in his *History of the Province of Massachusetts Bay*, which, with his published *Letters*, is still consulted. But by 1770 Thomas Hutchinson and his sons were consistent supporters of royal authority and far removed from the spirit of their famous progenitor, whose name is commemorated in the Hutchinson River and the Hutchinson River Parkway in Westchester County, New York, where she was killed by Siwanoy Indians.

Hutchinson approved the entry of British troops into

Boston, for by that time he considered the mobs out of hand and the executive powerless. In 1771 he was appointed Governor. During his short tenure occurred the Boston Tea Party, against which he was helpless. His usefulness in America was at an end when the patriots in 1773 published his confidential letters to British officials, in which he advocated curtailing the liberties of the colonials, his own countrymen. He resigned his office the next year and departed for London, where he died before the end of the Revolution.

SAMUEL ADAMS was the strongest antagonist Thomas Hutchinson had to face. He was the complete embodiment of the democratic will, just as Hutchinson was the frank exponent of royal prerogatives. Adams was the watchdog of the rights and privileges granted to the colonies in the first days of their settlement, and after the French and Indian War he analyzed every regulation imposed by the royal government, and explained its significance to the people. Hutchinson called him "the great incendiary." He was really the great instigator, for he was responsible for most of the protests voted by the Massachusetts House, for the direct appeals to the King and cabinet, for starting communications with the rest of the colonies and finally putting the Committees of Correspondence on a regular basis, leading to the Continental Congress.

Adams was born in Boston September 22, 1722, and in March, 1770, was 47 years old. He had been graduated in

1740 from Harvard, where he had studied theology. He preferred business experience, as a brewer and tax collector. From 1766 to 1774 he was recording clerk of the House (Assembly) of the Massachusetts General Court (legislature) and was instrumental in drawing up many of the official papers; in addition he used to write letters on current issues for the newspapers under assumed names. The Committees of Correspondence, by means of which Adams kept issues alive in towns and assemblies, were organized in 1772. Adams worked for a long time to force Parliament to revise its methods toward America, always preferring to use legal avenues of protest, but invariably defying the royal governor. He frequently asserted that he was not thinking of separating from England, although he never yielded in his defense of home rule under all circumstances. When he was accused of being a revolutionary, he retorted in 1765: "There is no struggling for independence. The contrary is most certainly true. There is no appearance of such a disposition. There never will be unless Great Britain shall exert her power to destroy their [colonies'] liberties."

Samuel Adams took a leading part in the Continental Congress, signed the Declaration of Independence, labored with the constitutional convention of Massachusetts, and eventually occupied the offices once held by the royal appointees, Francis Bernard and Thomas Hutchinson, whom he had fought. He was Lieutenant Governor 1789 to 1793, and Governor 1794 through 1797.

John Adams and Samuel Adams were second cousins. The two Adamses had great respect for each other, although they differed in temperament and in their reaction to events. John Adams had firm convictions about his duty to fight for the liberties and privileges of the public, both in specific cases and in the abstract, but he was intensely introspective, often concerned about the public's estimate of his actions. Samuel Adams was much more combative, ready at all times to urge the public to listen to him, convinced that his political ideas had to be forcefully presented. John Adams thought Samuel had the most thorough understanding of liberty and its resources in the temper and character of the people, though not in the law and the constitution on which John built his case; Samuel, he considered, had the most radical love of liberty of any of their associates, and wielded "the most correct, genteel and artful pen."

There is plenty of evidence of Samuel's skill as a polemicist; in his letters he presented his arguments with brevity and force, and if any correspondent ventured to challenge his views Adams was ready with a sharp retort before the ink was dry on the *Gazette*'s pages. Samuel, wrote John Adams, during the Stamp Act agitations, "is zealous, ardent, and keen in the cause; is always for softness, and delicacy, and prudence, where they will do, but is staunch and stiffly rigid and inflexible in the cause." Samuel had another trait that his friends seem to have taken for granted; he was tremendously industrious, and no man worked more diligently to pull all the elements of protest together into a powerful political force. But he could be quite unscrupulous when trying to gain his ends, as witness the misleading testimony about the Boston Massacre that he sent to England. There is no doubt that without him the pre-Revolutionary protests of Massachusetts would have been muted considerably.

William Tudor, who had been a law clerk in John

Adams' office, was writing a book in 1818 and applied to Adams for information about Samuel Adams. John was then 83 and living at Quincy. He seems to have detected a note of criticism in Tudor's letter, for he rose sharply to the defense of his former associate:

"You seem to wish me to write something to diminish the fame of Sam Adams, to show that he was not a man of profound learning, a great lawyer, a man of vast reading, a comprehensive statesman. In all this I shall not gratify you.

"Sam Adams, to my certain knowledge, from 1758 to 1775, that is for seventeen years, made it his constant rule to watch the rise of every brilliant genius, to seek his acquaintance, to court his friendship, to cultivate his natural feelings in favor of his native country, to warn him against the hostile designs of Great Britain, and to fix his affections and reflections on the side of his native country. . . . If Samuel Adams was not a Demosthenes in oratory, nor had half the learning of a Mansfield in law, or the universal history of a Burke, he had the art of commanding the learning, the oratory, the talents, the diamonds of the first water that his country afforded, without anybody knowing or suspecting he had but himself and a very few friends."

II   The Tragic Hours

****

1

The Affair at the Ropewalk

THE FIRST CLASH between civilians and soldiers took place on Friday, March 2, and left enough rancor and ill feeling to account for some of the provocation on the following Monday. It took place at John Gray's Ropewalk in the Fort Hill section, a long, narrow workshop for producing all kinds of cordage, and involved Sam Gray, one of the employees who seems to have been on hand wherever trouble was brewing. The original altercation is best described in the words of Nicholas Ferreter, who was present:

"On Friday Mr. John Gray told me to go to his Ropewalk to make some cables. I went and worked till about 12, and then I saw a soldier coming down the outside ropewalk, swearing, and saying he would have satisfaction. Before this there was one of our hands, while I was coiling a cable, said to a soldier: 'Do you want work?' 'Yes,' says the soldier, 'I do, faith'; 'Well' said he to the soldier, 'go clean my ———' [privy]. He [the soldier] damned us and made a blow at, and struck me. When I knocked up his neck his coat flew open and out dropped a naked cutlass, which I took up and carried off with me."

The soldier left, rallied his fellows and returned with about a dozen and attacked some workers, who called for help. "When they came to us," continued Ferreter, "we came up; then we had several knocks amongst us; at last they went off." So far this seems to have been a fist fight, but now the soldiers armed themselves with clubs, and in the afternoon they returned to renew the fight. This time John Gray stopped them. Ferreter recognized one of the soldiers as Matthew Killroy, who plays a major role in this crisis.

In the middle of this fracas John Hill identified himself as a member of the peace commission and "commanded peace." The soldiers were in no mood to listen. They made a lunge at Hill and missed; then they attacked an old man and cut him.

By this time the altercation had become a feud and the soldiers were thought to be stalking employees, evidently planning to catch one alone and give him a beating. One of the men who had been at the Ropewalk told Benjamin Burdick, with whom he boarded, that he believed himself in danger from soldiers "who had a spite at him." Burdick already had seen two soldiers near his house and caught one of them listening at a window.

"I saw him again near the house and asked him what he was after," said Burdick. "He said he was pumping ship. 'Was it not you that was hearkening at my window last night?' asked Burdick. " 'What if it was,' he said. I told him to march off and he damned me. I beat him till he had enough of it, and then he went off."

A few nights later when Burdick went out to join the crowd his wife told him to take his sword. "The reason for carrying the sword was: they spied the young man in the Lane and dogged him, for he had been very active in the affray at the Ropewalk, and they said they would some time or other have satisfaction, and I looked to myself to be liable to be insulted likewise."

"What passed at Mr. Gray's Ropewalk has already been given to the public" wrote the *Boston Gazette* on March 12 "and may be said to have led the way to the late catastrophe. That the Ropewalk lads, when attacked by superior numbers, should defend themselves with so much spirit and success in the clubway was too mortifying, and perhaps it may hereafter appear that even some of their officers were unhappily affected with this circumstance. Divers stories were propagated among the soldiery that served to agitate their spirits, particularly on the sabbath, that one Chambers, a sergeant, represented as a sober man, had been missing the preceding day, and must therefore have been murdered by the townsmen. An officer of distinction so far credited this report that he entered Mr. Gray's Ropewalk that sabbath, and when asked the occasion of his so doing, the officer replied it was to look if the sergeant, said to be murdered, had not been hid there. This sober sergeant was found on the Monday unhurt, in a house of pleasure."

The commanding officer of the 24th Regiment thought his men had been badly used. He brought a formal complaint to the Lieutenant Governor, mentioning the altercation at the Ropewalk and abuses in general by the townsmen. Hutchinson laid the complaint before the Council, but its members could not agree on what action to take.

The discipline of the British Army was sternly enforced, but the harsh penalties for infractions of the regulations made many privates bitter. The officers were well trained and most of them had bought their commissions, but among the men were many unemployable in civil occupations. The argument at Gray's Ropewalk seems to indicate there were hours when they could do menial work in the town. The temptation to desert and strike out for the far settlements must have been real, for one of the first proclamations read to the soldiers the week after their arrival offered a reward of ten guineas to the soldier "who should inform of any one who should attempt to seduce him from the service." Three days later "nine or ten" soldiers from Lieut. Colonel Carr's regiment were severely whipped on the Common by Negro drummers, their offenses not being named. The depositions by Bostonians record many instances of individual soldiers roaming the streets and intimidating civilians.

2

The Clash at Murray's Barracks

EARLY ON THE evening of March 5 trouble broke out at
Murray's Barracks between townsmen and soldiers. Two
townsmen, Francis Archbald and William Merchant, were
passing an alley that led to the barracks when they saw a
soldier brandishing a broadsword "of uncommon size," hit-
ting it against the stone walls and repeatedly striking fire.
With him was "a person of mean countenance," who carried a large cudgel. According to Archbald somebody said:
"Put up your cutlass; it is not right to carry it at this time
of night." The soldier said: "Damn you, ye Yankee boogers,
what's your business?" He struck Archibald on the arm and
then pierced Merchant's coat close to his armpit and
grazed the skin. Merchant struck the soldier with a short
stick he carried and the other man ran to the barracks for
help. He returned with several soldiers, one carrying a
pair of tongs and another a shovel. The first soldier fell
upon Archbald and hit him on the head with the tongs. A
lad named John Hicks arrived with others who had been

attracted by the noise and knocked the soldier down, and Archbald said quite blandly: "As he attempted to rise I struck him down again and broke his wrist, as I heard afterward."

The action became more general as newcomers joined the fray. The *Gazette* reported that "ten or twelve soldiers came out with clubs, cutlasses, and bayonets and fell upon the boys." They tried to make a stand but realizing "the inequality of their equipment" they dispersed.

Richard Palmes heard soldiers were abusing the inhabitants at the barracks and went down to investigate. He saw four or five soldiers with guns and bayonets. "I told the officer who stood by I was surprised they suffered the soldiers to be out at that time of night. He said: 'Do you pretend to teach us our duty, Sir?' I said 'No, only to remind you of it.' 'You see,' says he, 'the soldiers are in barracks. Why do you not go home?'" But the evening was young and Palmes became interested in the people in King Street.

Henry Bass was at Boylston Alley about 9 o'clock and saw only boys and children, 12 to 15 years old, some with walking canes. He said four soldiers with drawn cutlasses came out of the alley; "they fell on these boys and everybody else that came in their way; they struck them; they followed me and almost overtook me. I turned and saw an oysterman, who said to me, 'Damn it, here is what I have got by going up,' showing me his shoulder wound. I put my finger into the wound and bloodied it very much. This affair of the oysterman gathered numbers; before that there were not above eight, all little lads; in a little time I imagine about twenty gathered."

Dr. Richard Hirons was near the barracks when a soldier came out of the gate, knelt down in the middle of the street, and pointing his gun said: "Now, damn your bloods, I will make a lane through you all."

The action now changed to Samuel Atwood, who had enough curiosity to enter the alley from Dock Square to investigate. As soldiers came rushing down the alley to the Square he asked them if they intended to murder people. "Yes, by God root and branch!" was the reply. Thereupon one of the soldiers struck Atwood with a club, another did the same. As Atwood turned to leave, a third wounded him on the left shoulder down to the bone, causing him much pain. Retreating, he met two officers and asked, somewhat ingenuously, "Gentlemen, what is the matter?" They replied: "You'll see by and by."

The reporter for the *Gazette* recorded their subsequent activities, but his writing is so obviously colored that it reflects the animosities of the hour:

"Immediately after those heroes appeared in the Square, asking: 'Where are the boogers?' 'Where are the cowards?' But notwithstanding their fierceness to naked [unarmed] men, one of them advanced towards a youth who had a split of a raw stave in his hand and said: 'Damn them, here is one of them' but the young man, seeing a person near him with a drawn sword and a good cane ready to support him, held up his stave in defiance and they quietly passed by him up the little alley by Mr. Siliby's to King Street, where they attacked single and unarmed persons till they raised much clamor, and then turned down Cornhill Street, insulting all they met in like manner, and pursuing some to their very doors."

Captain John Goldfinch of the 14th Fuseliers was the officer who arrived in time to order the soldiers back into their barracks. When asked later whether the soldiers had cutlasses, he replied: "By no means." He had met some officers of the 29th Regiment and told them he suspected there would be a riot. "As I was the oldest officer I ordered the men to the barracks and they were immediately confined. The mob followed me and came to the gate of the barracks and abused the men very much indeed with bad language, so that the men must have been enraged very much."

3

The Riot in King Street

✻

A BARBER'S apprentice with a grievance on behalf of his employer touched off the sequence of events that ended in stark tragedy on the night of March 5, 1770. Captain John Goldfinch, an officer in the 14th Regiment of West Yorkshire Fuseliers, was passing by in King Street when a barber's boy called out: "There goes the fellow who hath not paid my master for dressing his hair."

A sentry, Hugh Montgomery of the 29th Worcestershire, who was pacing up and down in front of the Custom House steps, replied, according to Goldfinch's temperate account: "He is a gentleman, and if he owes you anything he will pay for it."

"Fortunately for me I had his receipt in my pocket," said Goldfinch. "I passed on without taking any notice of what the boy said."

There were other townsmen in King Street whose accounts contradict this polite exchange. They said the boy was insistent, and after he had demanded payment several times the sentry pushed him so roughly out of the way that he knocked him down. The boy picked himself up and shouted to a gathering group: "There is the son of a bitch that knocked me down!"

The response from the crowd was immediately hostile: "Kill him! Kill him! Knock him down!" Such cries, permeating the clear night air, started loiterers in their direction. People began to gather across the gutter from the sentry. They were mostly young fellows, aged around 18 or in the early 20's. "Bloody lobster back!" was their favorite insult. They traded accounts of lobster backs beaten up by town boys. They told of a fracas at Murray's Barracks only an hour before, with a British officer driving the soldiers back into their quarters.

The situation at the Custom House was growing tense. The people were taunting the sentry, and not merely calling names; they were picking up pieces of ice and tossing them at him. The crowd was getting larger. About twenty or so, many of whom appeared to be sailors, approached from Cornhill. They were led by a tall mulatto, who was carrying a large cord wood stick. They were shouting and whistling, and seven or eight were carrying their sticks over their heads.

James Bailey walked up to the sentry to find out what was going on. He saw pieces of ice "hard and large enough to hurt any man, as big as one's fist," thrown at the sentry, who said he was afraid that if the boys did not disperse there would be "something" very soon, but he did not define it.

A tall 19-year-old fellow named Henry Knox joined the crowd from Cornhill; he had heard exaggerated reports about the affair at Murray's Barracks. Since the age of 9 he had been working in the bookstore of Wharton & Bowes in Cornhill, and in his spare time he drilled with an artillery company. He thought he saw a crowd of one hundred and fifty to two hundred, and when he asked what was up was told that a number of soldiers had been out "with bayonets and cutlasses and had attacked and cut the people all the way down Cornhill and then retreated to their barracks; one fellow said they had been "cutting fore and aft."

When Knox approached King Street the sentry was loading his gun and the people said he was going to fire. He had taken a defensive stance and was waving his gun about, and held it in the position for a bayonet charge. Knox told him that if he fired he must die for it; the sentry said damn them, if they molested him he would fire. Boys, about 17 or 18 according to Knox, were yelling "Fire and be damned!" Knox resented the badgering of the sentry. "I tried to keep one fellow off from the sentinel," he explained afterward, "and either struck him or pushed him away." He identified a lad named Usher as having said: "God damn him, we will knock him down for snapping."

About this time the crowd in King Street was augmented by stragglers coming in from Dock Square, where a man in a red cloak and white wig had been seen haranguing a group. Nobody knew who he was, but all listened attentively to what he had to say, and since they came away from him in a truculent mood it was assumed that he had denounced the military.

David Mitchelson thought there was a large crowd, about two hundred, in Dock Square, and said the man "made a considerable figure there." William Hunter said he was a tall man who talked to the people for some time; "then he took off, and they took off their hats and gave three cheers for the main guard." Mitchelson also said they "huzza'd for the main guard," but James Selkring, who also saw the man in the red cloak, does not mention any huzzas or call for the guard. None of them could repeat what the speaker said, but the huzzas indicated he was stirring up trouble.

Who was the man and what did he have to say? The presumption is that he was talking against the soldiers. The red cloak and white wig were a sort of badge of distinction, which men who had held high office were accustomed to wear. This suggests that the speaker was a person of some authority. Yet none of the witnesses or the newspapers gave his name.

The situation was getting worse and Montgomery, the sentry, was alarmed. Benjamin Lee, who was standing beside him and had heard the taunts of the barber's boy, saw the sentry go up to the door of the Custom House and knock with the butt of his gun, but could not get in; then he turned, primed and loaded, and levelled his gun with his hip, and told the people to stand off. But Josiah Simpson was also present and saw the sentry give "three large and remarkable strokes" on the door with the brass knocker, and talk to someone who opened the door. What makes these discrepancies in observation—memories of past experiences? But the spectators all agreed that Montgomery had shouted:

"Turn out, Main Guard!"

And the main guard came. Thomas Wilkinson said it appeared "as it were from behind the old Brick Meeting House" (Old South) and heard Captain Thomas Preston, Officer of the Day, yell: "Turn out, damn your bloods, turn out!" They were evidently unprepared, for several who tumbled out had no coats on, "cursing and damning like wild creatures." As they hurried into King Street, followed by Captain Preston, with laced hat and drawn sword, they pushed the people roughly aside. The crowd yelled and whistled through their fingers. Evidently Preston put the soldiers through a spurt of discipline, for Josiah Simpson recalled that the officer ordered: "Handle your arms! Ease your arms! Recover your arms! Support your arms! Prime and load!"

He was the only member of the crowd who recalled this, and his questioner seemed a bit skeptical and asked: "Are you certain he said all that?"

"I am as certain as I am of my own existence."

Montgomery joined the soldiers and the eight lined up in a sort of half circle and faced the crowd. Captain Preston stood behind them.

The soldiers who were lined up were sufficient to protect the sentry, but to the mob they presented a new challenge. The soldiers were now in the position of a chained bear that is being baited by spectators crowding ever closer to its claws. The mob was able to enrage the soldiers by calling them names and daring them to shoot, feeling confident they would not do so.

The shouts that had greeted the soldiers now changed to threats and imprecations. "Lobsters!" "Bloody backs!" "How much for lobsters?" And a shower of snowballs, pieces of ice—some as big as a man's fist, oyster shells, and lumps of sea coal, some of the missiles striking the guns of the men.

The taunts were sarcastic. Cowards, you need guns to face unarmed men? Put your guns down and we're your men!

A man boosted a boy into a window of the Brick Meeting House and told him to pull the bell rope. The bell set up a clangor that meant only one thing to Boston—fire! Householders picked up their leather water-buckets and dashed out. But when bells in other steeples joined the noise some men suspected a riot rather than a fire and reached for a cutlass. Nothing more was needed to swell the crowds in King Street.

Many voices were crying: "Fire! Why don't you fire?" and maybe someone gave the order to fire, although this was never established. Six shots came, not in a volley but in spurts, and when the smoke cleared three men lay dead in King Street, with leaden balls from the double-loaded muskets in their bodies. Two, fatally wounded, died later; six others were injured. The dead were Crispus Attucks, a 47-year-old mulatto, part Negro, part Indian, lately from New Providence and apparently going to sea; Samuel Gray, worker from Gray's Ropewalk; James Caldwell, mate on Captain Morton's vessel, hit by two balls in chest, and Samuel Maverick, 17-year-old apprentice to an ivory turner, hit in the torso. Patrick Carr, badly wounded, died ten days later. The other wounded were John Clark, 17, an apprentice; Christopher Monk, 17, shipwright's apprentice; David Parker, wheelwright's apprentice; Robert Patterson, "a seafaring man, who was the person that had his trousers shot through in Richardson's affair"; Edward Payne, a merchant, who received a ball in his arm while standing at his front door, and John Green, a tailor, hit while coming up Leverett's Lane.

As Dr. Gardner and a man named Brinkly came forward to pick up Attucks and Gray the soldiers presented their arms as if they were going to fire again, when Captain Preston pushed up their guns and said: "Stop firing! Do not fire!" The crowd, shocked and demoralized, scattered as men hurried to the victims. John Cox's outburst of anger must have been typical, for as he helped pick up the dead he told the soldiers that it was a cowardly trick to kill men within reach of their bayonets who had nothing in their hands. Cox said the officer replied: "Damn you, fire again and let them take the consequences," whereupon Cox said: "You have killed ——— [enough?] already to hang you all." It is doubtful that the retort came from Captain Preston.

The erratic firing by the soldiers resulted from that break in human endurance that comes when men not responsible for their situation are goaded into a desperate response to their tormentors.

The regimental drums beat to arms and the 29th Regiment under Lieut. Colonel Carr formed three divisions near the northeast corner of the main guard. The first division took a kneeling position for street fighting in front of the northeast corner of the Town House. The 14th Regiment was placed under arms but remained in its barracks.

Lieutenant Governor Hutchinson was in his house when the bells began to ring and word of the shooting reached him. He hurried down to King Street, where he was met by an angry crowd shouting for him to do something. He confronted Captain Preston and demanded: "Do you know, sir, you have no power to fire on any body of the people collected together except you have a civil magistrate with you to give orders?" Although Samuel Adams and several others said Preston replied: "I was obliged to, to save the sentry," or "I did it to save my sentry," the Hutchinson report, published by his son, reads: "The noise was so great that his answer could not be understood."

Propelled toward the Town House Hutchinson went upstairs and found several members of the Council and a number of civil magistrates already there. He was followed by members of the crowd who, according to the *Gazette*, "expressed themselves to his honor with a freedom and warmth becoming the occasion." Hutchinson did his utmost to assure them that justice would be done. Importuned to address the crowd outside he stepped out on the little balcony that overlooked the place where Attucks and Gray had fallen, and asked for quiet. He said that a terrible tragedy had befallen them and asked all to disperse and go home quietly, promising to do all in his power to see that justice would be done. He said: "Let the law have its course. I will live and die by the law."

But the crowd wanted stronger assurances; it wanted Captain Preston and his squad arrested and the 29th Regiment, which was drawn up under arms, sent back to its barracks. Hutchinson indicated that this was beyond his authority, but Lieut. Colonel William Dalrymple agreed this should be done and gave the order. Several cooler heads urged the crowd to leave, warning against the danger of a rash engagement during the night and saying that measures taken next morning would be more likely to obtain satisfaction for the spilled blood of their fellow-townsmen. The people thereupon began to leave.

After midnight Justices Richard Dania and John Tudor gave a warrant to the High Sheriff calling on him to produce Captain Preston for interrogation at the Town House. The examination started at 2 o'clock, and Judge John Tudor noted that "we sent him to gaol soon after 3, having evidence sufficient to commit him on his ordering the soldiers to fire."

In the hours before dawn King Street was deserted. The brawl of March 5, 1770, was passing into history, but the blood on the cobbles in front of the Custom House would become indelible.

4

Not One Regiment, But Two

ON TUESDAY MORNING the atmosphere of Boston was tense and expectant. Sons of Liberty were coming into town over Boston Neck, ready for trouble. The reporter for the *Gazette* drew on his imagination to describe a scene observed by no one else when he wrote: "Tuesday morning presented a most shocking scene, the blood of our fellow citizens running like water through King Street and the Merchants Exchange, the principal spot of the military parade for about 18 months past. Our blood might also be tracked up to the head of Long Lane, and through divers other streets and passages."

A town meeting had been called for that morning at Faneuil Hall, and when John Hancock opened it at 11 o'clock the place was crowded by people who approved the demands of speakers that the military occupation of Boston end at once. They appointed a committee of fifteen, with Samuel Adams as chairman, to present a resolution to that effect to Lieutenant Governor Hutchinson, who was also meeting that morning with the Council and Colonel Dalrymple, commander in chief of the two regiments, in Town Hall. The resolution read:

> That it is the unanimous opinion of this meeting that the inhabitants and soldiery can no longer live together in safety; that nothing can rationally be expected to restore the peace of the town and prevent further blood and carnage but the immediate removal of the troops; and that we therefore must fervently pray his honor that his power and influence may be asserted for their instant removal.

While Adams and his committee went to the Town Hall, the public meeting was transferred to Old South Meeting House, which could hold more spectators. To them Hutchinson replied:

> I am extremely sorry for the unhappy differences between the inhabitants and troops, and especially for the action of the last evening, and I have exerted myself upon that occasion that a due enquiry may be made, and that the law may have its course. I have in Council consulted with the commanding officers of the two regiments who are in the town. They have their orders from the General at New York. It is not in my power to countermand those orders. The Council have desired that the two regiments may be removed to the Castle. From the particular concern which the 29th Regiment has had in your differences, Colonel Dalrymple, who is the commanding officer of the troops, has signified that that regiment shall without delay be placed in the barracks at the Castle until he can send to the General and receive his further orders concerning both the regiments, and that the main guard shall be removed, and the 14th Regiment so disposed and laid under such restraint that all occasion of future differences may be prevented.

The Lieutenant Governor's reply was read to the audience of more than 4,000 people packed into Old South, and when the question was asked, should the offer be accepted, there was a resounding "No!" and only one "Yes." The meeting then appointed Samuel Adams, John Hancock, William Molineux, William Phillips, Dr. Joseph Warren, Joshua Henshaw, and Samuel Pemberton a new committee to wait on the Lieutenant Governor, Colonel Dalrymple and the Council to convey the information that the reply was not satisfactory and that nothing would satisfy the town but the "total and immediate removal of all the troops." The shouted demand "Not one, but two!" expressed the determination of the townsmen.

This time Hutchinson was aware that Samuel Adams spoke not for himself alone but for the whole community. When he again replied that he did not have authority to proceed further, Adams pointed out that such power was granted in the charter of the Province. He did not know— nor did anyone until the papers of General Gage reached the William Clements Library at Ann Arbor, Mich., 150 years later—that Gage had given the civil power the use of the troops. Adams now firmly rebuted Hutchinson: "Sir, if the Lieutenant Governor or Colonel Dalrymple, or both together, have authority to remove one regiment, they have authority to remove two, and nothing short of a total evacuation of the town, by all the regular troops, will satisfy the public mind or preserve the peace of the Province." Samuel Adams had the satisfaction of seeing Hutchinson's knees tremble. "I thought I saw his face grow pale" said Adams, "and I enjoyed the sight."

The Lieutenant Governor placed the petition of the town before the Council and asked its advice; the Council replied unanimously that it was absolutely necessary for his majesty's service, the good order of the town, and the peace of the Province, that the troops be removed immediately out of Boston. Thereupon Colonel Dalrymple informed the committee "that he now gave his word of honor that he would begin his preparations in the morning, and that there should be no unnecessary delay until the whole of the two regiments had been removed to the Castle." This decision was received by the town meeting with joyous acclaim.

The leaders were determined there should be no occasion for violent clashes between soldiers and townsmen before the regiments were safely housed in the barracks at Castle William. The colonel of the Boston militia informed Hutchinson that he wished to set a watch to patrol the streets, and Hutchinson gave a hesitant assent, then told the colonel he doubted he had the authority to order one. This was too much for the exasperated colonel, who promptly told the Governor off. Hutchinson replied he would not forbid the watch but recommended care. He said later he had "appointed a watch." The colonel enrolled volunteers for night duty, and one of those who armed and walked the streets for several hours every evening was John Adams, who recorded this in his diary.

The troops marched to their boats in military order, to the great delight of small boys and the taunts of bystanders. Samuel Adams observed that the removal of the troops was in the slowest order, taking eleven days, when it had taken only fortyeight hours to land them. Later, soldiers and their families were permitted to come into Boston for provisions, and met with no molestation. In London they were called "Sam Adams' two regiments."

Protests from the aroused citizens of Massachusetts towns reached the Lieutenant Governor. Typical was the action of Roxbury, which on March 8 petitioned Hutchinson for the removal of all troops, desiring "in a peculiar manner," to express "astonishment, grief and indignation at the horrid and barbarous action committed there last Monday evening by a party of these troops."

After the town meeting had obtained the promise of Colonel Dalrymple that he would remove the soldiers, its committee went busily to work to prepare an account of the massacre for the enlightenment of high officials of the British Government and supporters of the American position in London. But industrious as they were, they were anticipated by the Hutchinson administration, which rushed reports and letters to England in the royal frigate that sailed March 16. The documents were carried by John Robinson, the Commissioner of Customs who was particularly hated by the public as the man who had wounded James Otis, Jr., severely by blows on the head during an altercation in a coffee house. Robinson paid damages, but Otis refused to accept them. The injury was supposed to have brought about Otis' later madness.

The pamphlet prepared by the town committee was called *A Short Narrative of the Horrid Massacre in Boston* and was filled with the depositions of 96 witnesses of the events on the evening of March 5. The object was to demonstrate that the royal troops had been on a wild rampage for weeks. Samuel Adams certainly believed the soldiers guilty of murder without any extenuation, as his letters to the newspapers and other public activities showed. It was a question whether his methods were above reproach, but only his royalist enemies asked that. The *Narrative* was withheld from publication in Boston in order not to influence prospective jurors in the coming trials of the soldiers.

The men who gathered the depositions of witnesses to the shooting were not critical of what was told them; probably they urged the spectators to elaborate on their experiences. The result was a collection of statements in which gossip and conjecture played a large part. Many of the witnesses attributed the shooting to orders by Captain Preston and mentioned frequent wild outbreaks by soldiers, who attacked civilians with clubs and cutlasses. It was not until some of these men were interrogated in court seven months later that they modified their positive conclusions, and a more balanced account of what took place came to light. The committee of the town meeting, however, wanted to make a strong case against use of the military and offset the charge of mob rule sent to London by the royal party.

So many witnesses told the committee that they had heard threats of a concerted attack on the people by the soldiers that the committee's report strongly implied that a massacre of the inhabitants was in the making. Individual soldiers who threatened to get even with civilians were lumped together to give the impression of a conspiracy. For example, William Newhall swore he heard a soldier of the 24th Regiment say there were a great many "that would eat their dinners on Monday next, that should not eat on Tuesday." Daniel Calfe heard the wife of James McDeed, a soldier of the 29th Regiment, say that before Tuesday or Wednesday night they would wet their swords and bayonets in New England peoples' blood.

Ten days before the massacre John Wilme told David Cockran not to be out of the house on a certain day because there would be disturbances. A soldier took him by the arm and said blood would soon run in the streets of Boston. Sarah Wilme reported that Christian Rowley of the 14th Regiment had said the soldiers were to march up King Street and he would level his piece not to miss; however, women and others who sided with the soldiers would be taken to Castle William for protection. Other threats by soldiers during the earlier clashes with the town boys, spoken in the heat of battling, were recalled and given sinister significance the day after the massacre.

The committee also published the report that Captain Wilson of the 59th Regiment urged the Negroes to "take away their masters' lives and property and repair to the army for protection, which was fully proved against him."

While Captain Wilson may well have made such a statement, and soldiers may have circulated some alarming rumors to satisfy their self-importance, the charge of conspiracy was not pursued at the trials.

The worst act of misrepresentation in a deposition was perpetrated by Samuel Drowne. Drowne swore that he saw flashes from two guns fired from the Custom House, one out of a window of a room west of the balcony, the other from the balcony. His remarks led to the arrest and indictment for murder of four men who were fully innocent. They were subject to the indignities of prison and the suspicions of their fellows before the jury dismissed the charge. Although Drowne was lying the Boston committee accepted his assertions as truth and included them in the account it sent to London. The artist who drew the sketch of the massacre for Paul Revere's engraving accepted his version and included the firing from the Custom House.

The Hutchinson *History* comments: "The variance of their account of the facts from the statement of the whole evidence as it appeared afterward at the trials is a strong instance of the small dependence which can be placed upon witnesses examined by men engaged in political controversy."

Hutchinson became most apprehensive of what the Boston populace might do. He had personally suffered from mob violence; his house had been ransacked and many objects that contributed to his feeling for elegant living had been destroyed. Now he felt he had lost control. Colonel Dalrymple observed his perturbation and concluded Hutchinson was without friends and without power. Hutchinson was in such low spirits two weeks after the massacre that he thought nobody dared oppose the public, that "in matters of dispute between the King and colonies government is at an end and in the hands of the people." General Gage later wrote Lord Hillsborough that Boston and its government had been influenced for a long time by "mad people"; that actually there was little government in Boston.

The town committee, led by Samuel Adams, wanted an immediate trial of the accused soldiers; the administration worked to delay action as long as possible. A town meeting held in Faneuil Hall on March 19 drew up a letter to the Lieutenant Governor asking for the appointment of special justices to hear the trials of the accused soldiers. They said that seamen who were material witnesses "in the late tragical murder in Boston" were being detained to their great disadvantage. The Lieutenant Governor, however, was determined there should be no early trials. On this issue he and John Adams were in agreement; they did not want the soldiers tried while passions were still hot. Both were fearful of a popular demonstration. Hutchinson's excuse for delaying the trial was "so that people may have time to cool," and actually he and other Crown officials feared a quick trial would result in conviction for murder and execution of the soldiers. This also was the fear of Captain Preston. When advices from the London government reached Hutchinson late in April, he found that officials there had similar apprehensions, and he was informed that if the soldiers were convicted they were to be reprieved and pardoned by the King.

Samuel Adams and his associates were extremely suspicious of any reports sent to London by Acting Governor Hutchinson and the Commissioners of Customs. When John Robinson was rushed off to London with their letters Adams protested that the contents "of a public nature," and the names of their signers, should be made public. On July 10 Benjamin Franklin became Agent in London for the Province, following the death of DeBerdt. Adams wrote him that he was pleased to learn that the *Short Narrative*, which the town meeting had authorized, was "establishing the truth in the minds of honest men" and refuting charges that the Boston people had been the aggressors on March 5. But he was astonished to learn that Parliament was giving credence to "garbled reports" contained in letters from America written by persons with wicked intentions toward the colonies. The Boston leaders were determined to continue to fight their bad press abroad. With this in view a town meeting on July 10 appointed a new committee, on which appeared such familiar names as Adams, Hancock, Cushing, Dana and Joseph Warren, to prepare a report on the "true state" of the town and acts of the Commissioners of Customs since March 5.

It was called *Additional Observations to a Short Narrative of the Horrid Massacre in Boston.*

Charles Lucas, editor of the *Freeman's Journal,* is supposed to have met Benjamin Franklin when the latter visited Ireland. He wrote the Boston committee on the massacre, James Bowdoin and Dr. Joseph Warren, comparing the plight of America to that of Ireland. He said: "What redress do you expect for grievances in America, which are grown familiar in England and almost the established, the sole mode of government in Ireland?"

5

The Case of Crispus Attucks

A NEW APOTHEOSIS awaits Crispus Attucks. After 200 years, during which his name never quite dropped out of mention, the movement to recognize the accomplishments of the American Negro assures him new prominence. James Baldwin, the novelist, brought him to the attention of certain members of Congress in Washington, who seemed at a loss to identify him. But the biggest praise has come from a white writer, William Loren Katz, who calls Attucks "the first martyr of the American Revolution."

Katz is an editor and historian, who has lectured for the Department of Education of the State of New York, and whose book, *Eye Witness: the Negro in American History*, is a comprehensive encyclopedia describing Negroes who took part in the nation's battles or became leaders in political and social life, and in the arts. He presents a full-page drawing of the massacre, which shows Attucks in the middle foreground receiving the full blast from a British grenadier's musket in his chest. The drawing differs considerably from Paul Revere's famous engraving, for it shows clubs in the hands of the civilians, something completely ignored by Revere's artist. Katz inflates the shooting his own way by calling it the first battle of the Revolution. There have been numerous other claims to that distinction, and although the fracas in King Street no doubt germinated thoughts of revolt, the real incentive was to get the soldiers out of Boston, not to break with England.

Who was Crispus Attucks? The first printed identification of him appeared in the *Boston Gazette* for March 12, 1770, the issue that describes "this horrid Massacre." It says the dead included "a mulatto man, named Crispus Attucks, who was born in Framingham, but lately belonged to New Providence and was here in order to go to North Carolina . . ." In the transcript of testimony given at the trial of the British soldiers Attucks is repeatedly spoken of as a mulatto. Only in one instance, in the interrogation of a witness, is he referred to as an Indian.

The term mulatto, meaning a person of mixed racial parentage, has fallen into disuse, but 100 years ago it was applied quite freely to one of white and Negro parentage. In writings of that time one sees references to quadroon and octoroon to indicate ethnic differences, and audiences went to the theater to see *The Octoroon* and weep over the hard lot of a beautiful girl with a mixed ancestry.

Information about Crispus Attucks' earlier years was published by Frederick Kidder in his centennial *History of the Boston Massacre* in 1870. He wrote:

"Crispus Attucks is described as a mulatto; he was born in Framingham near the Chochituate Lake and not far from the line of Natick. Here an old cellar hole remains where the Attucks family formerly lived. Attucks is an Indian word meaning a deer and was often given to children; his ancestors were probably of the Natick tribe, who had intermarried with Negroes who were slaves, and as their descendants were held as such, he inherited their condition, although it is likely the blood of three races coursed through his veins."

If Attucks is an Indian word it may be surmised that it was the man's father who was an Indian.

There was also something to be gleaned from the press, in this case the Framingham and Boston papers of October, 1750. "It would seem that this event was not his first effort for liberty," comments Kidder, "for twenty years before he had run away from his master, who published in the *Boston Gazette or Weekly Journal* the following description of him, which shows that he must have been about 47 at the time he was killed:

"Run away from his master, William Brown of Framingham, on the 27th of September last, a mulatto fellow about 27 years of age, named Crispus, 6 feet, 2 inches high, short curled hair, his knees nearer together than common; had on a light-colored beaverskin coat, new buckskin breaches, blue yarn stockings and a checked woollen shirt. Whoever shall take up said runaway and convey him to the aforesaid master shall have 10 pounds old livre reward and all necessary charges paid; and all masters of vessels and others are hereby cautioned against concealing or carrying off said servant on penalty of the law."

It was undoubtedly this notice that led Mrs. Catherine Drinker Bowen to describe Attucks, in *John Adams and the American Revolution*, as "the huge knock-kneed mulatto of 47 who seemed to have done more rioting than any other six men together."

Attucks` place as a leader of a group was described in great detail by Andrew, the servant of the Wendell family. It is told in the chapter on the soldiers' trial. Attucks must have carried a fairly long stick, for John Danbrooke said: "The mulatto was leaning on a long stick he had, resting his breast upon it."

A number of spectators described Attucks as having brandished a cord stick. James Bailey said: "I saw a number going up Cornhill and this mulatto fellow headed them." About twenty or thirty appeared to be sailors, some had sticks, some had none.

"Which way was the mulatto with his party going when you saw them?"

"Right towards the town pump."

"What did the party with the mulatto do or say?"

"They were huzzaing, whistling and carrying their sticks upright over their heads."

"What number of sticks?"

"Seven or eight, I suppose."

Bailey, who said Montgomery fired the first gun, imagined that Montgomery killed Attucks. Attucks was about fifteen feet away from him across the gutter. Bailey said somebody struck Montgomery, but it was not Attucks.

Patrick Keaton swore that he saw the tall mulatto fellow with two clubs in his hands, who said to him: "Here, take one of them. I did so. They were cord wood sticks. I went up to the head of the Lane and I dropped the stick in the snow; he went on cursing and swearing at the soldiers."

Ebenezer Bridgham saw about twelve men with sticks in their hands stand in the middle of the street. They gave three cheers and immediately surrounded the soldiers, "and struck upon their guns with their sticks, and passed along the front of the soldiers towards Royal Exchange Lane, striking the soldiers' guns as they passed."

"Did they seem to be sailors or townsmen?"

"They were dressed, some of them, in the habits of sailors." When Bridgham was asked whether he saw a mulatto among them, he replied: "I did not observe."

Then there was James Brewer, who contradicted a number of witnesses:

"Did you see a party of people like sailors coming down from Jackson's Corner with sticks?"

"No. I saw none."

"When you first saw the mulatto, did you hear him say anything to the soldiers or strike at them?"

"No."

"Had he a stick or club?"

"No."

Crispus Attucks played an important role in the trial of the British soldiers. There John Adams, defense counsel, chose Attucks as the principal aggressor:

"Attucks appeared to have undertaken to be the hero of the night, and to lead this army with banners, to form them in the first place in Dock Square, and march them up to King Street with their clubs. They passed through the main street up to the main guard in order to make the attack. If this was not an unlawful assembly, there never was one . . .

"Now to have this reinforcement coming down under the command of a stout mulatto fellow, whose very looks were enough to frighten any person, what had not the soldiers then to fear? He had hardiness enough to fall in upon them, and with one hand took hold of a bayonet, and with the other knocked the man down. This was the behavior of

Attucks, to whose mad proceedings in probability the dreadful carnage of that night was chiefly to be ascribed. And it was in this manner this town had been often treated; a Carr from Ireland, and an Attucks from Framingham, happening to be here, sally out upon their thoughtless enterprise . . ."

In this instance the two Adamses were at opposite poles. Samuel Adams contradicted everything John Adams said and became the most earnest defender of Attucks in writing to the *Boston Gazette*. It is true that he also was using Attucks for a purpose—to deny the soldiers had any justification for firing, and to keep the people aroused against the military. His line of argument is not very convincing. He asserted that although witnesses said they had seen Attucks with a club, "and great pains were taken to make it appear that he attacked the soldiers," the proof failed. "Even Andrew, a Negro witness, testifies that he thought Attucks was the man who struck one of the soldiers, but could not account how he could get at such a distance as he was when he fell, the soldier firing so soon. Others swear that he was leaning on his stick when he fell, which certainly was not a threatening posture. It may be supposed that he had as good a right to carry a stick, even a bludgeon, as the soldier who shot him had to be armed with musket and ball, and if he at any time lifted up his weapon of defense it was surely not more than a soldier's levelling his gun at the multitude charged with death."

Boston had more compassion and help for the Negro than any other American city, and long before it fought the Fugitive Slave Law it had elevated Attucks to the place of a martyr to liberty. However, as one generation succeeded another, the exact location of the common grave of the five victims of the Boston Massacre was forgotten; it was considered sufficient to know that they were in the patriots' Valhalla, the Old Granary Burying Ground. When the time came to revere them anew a memorial was placed on Boston Common in 1888 and Attucks' name inscribed thereon. John Fiske, the historian, made the address, and John Boyle O'Reilly celebrated the event in verse. In the 20th century Attucks achieved inclusion in the *Dictionary of American Biography*, in the same volume that celebrated the achievements of John and Samuel Adams.

6

Patrick Carr Was Ready for a Fight

❈

PATRICK CARR, the fifth man to die from a bullet wound received on the evening of March 5, proved by his behavior before the clash that he had expected trouble and was ready to take part in it. His ire rose when he heard the original alarm, which most people thought was for a fire, but which he decided called for a sword. Mrs. Catherine Field, his landlady, and her husband detained him.

"When the bells rung he went upstairs and put his surtout on," said Mrs. Field, "and got a hangar and put it betwixt his coat and surtout. My husband coming in at that time gave him a push and felt the sword; he wanted to take it from him, but he (Carr) was not willing to let it go. My husband told him he should not take it with him. I do not know what he said, but one of the neighbors was in the house, coaxed the sword out of his hand, and he went on without it."

When Carr was shot down his friends picked him up and carried him back to Mrs. Field's house. At about 11 o'clock they called Dr. John Jeffries, the surgeon, but Jeffries was attending another case at that hour, and it was not until the next morning that, in company with others, Dr. Jeffries saw Carr and dressed his wounds.

The entry of Dr. Jeffries into this case had unexpected results, for he was called on later to testify at the trial of the soldiers, and as he had Tory sympathies it is quite evident that his partisan views were reflected in his testimony. Dr. Lloyd, who was present, said to him: "Jeffries, I believe this man will be able to tell us how the affair was; we had better ask him." Jeffries thereupon discovered an unusual compassion for the abused soldiers in this Irishman who had gone out to fight them and had been hurt.

"I advised him never to go again into quarrels and riots," said Dr. Jeffries; "he said he was very sorry he did go. I asked him then how long he had been in King Street when they fired. He said he went from Mr. Field's when the bells rung; when he got to Walker's corner, saw many persons coming from Cornhill, who, he was told, had been quarreling with the soldiers down there; that he went with them as far as the stocks; that he stopped there, but they passed on. While he was standing there he saw many things thrown at the sentry.

"I asked him if he knew what was thrown. He said he heard the things strike against the guns, as they sounded hard; he believed they were oyster shells and ice; he heard the people huzza every time they heard anything strike that sounded hard; that he then saw some soldiers going down towards the Custom House; that he saw the people pelt them as they went along. After they had got down there he crossed over toward Warden and Vernon's shop in order to see what they would do, that as he was passing he was shot . . ."

Dr. Jeffries prodded Carr to determine whether the soldiers "were abused a great deal" and Carr said he thought they were. Did he think the soldiers would fire, and Carr replied he thought the soldiers would have fired long before. Would the soldiers have been hurt if they had not fired? Carr said he thought they would, that he had heard many voices cry out: "Kill them!"

Another reason why Carr thought the soldiers would shoot lay in his own experience. As Dr. Jeffries reported it: "He told me also that he was a native of Ireland, that he had frequently seen mobs, and soldiers called upon to quell them; he had seen soldiers often fire on the people in Ireland, but in his life had never seen them bear half so much before they fired."

Thus Dr. Jeffries made quite clear that Carr thought the soldiers had been badly abused before they fired. He described Carr as a remorseful fellow, who would interrupt his account to call himself a fool and say he might have known better. In his extremity he told Dr. Jeffries that he forgave the man who shot him, whoever he was; he was satisfied the soldier had no malice but fired to defend himself.

This deathbed testimony was reported at the trial of the British soldiers and may well have helped them out of their plight. It is, however, subject to a reservation. Dr. John Jeffries was hardly an objective witness. He was respected as a physician, and was not active in politics, but his Tory leanings became clear later, beginning with his service as a surgeon to the British troops at Bunker Hill. He chose to remain in Boston during the siege, and when General

William Howe and his troops departed Dr. Jeffries went with them. He established a practice in London, but eventually resumed his residence in the United States, and living well into the nineteenth century, was known to Dr. Oliver Wendell Holmes.

On Thursday, March 8, Boston reverently buried the first four victims of the massacre. No one could recall when there had been such a huge gathering of Boston citizens; the crowd was estimated at 3,000. It was such an occasion for demonstrations of emotion that all Crown officials and military had best keep indoors. All shops closed their doors; all movement of goods in the harbor stopped. The bells of the churches rang in slow tempo and similar tones drifted across the river from Charlestown, and from the spires of Braintree and other towns in the environs.

The hearses moved in separate processions to meet in King Street, where the men had died, and then proceeded to the Granary Burying Ground. The procession was in columns of six abreast, followed by coaches carrying the well-to-do. Attucks and Caldwell, having no homes in Boston, had been lying in Faneuil Hall; Gray was at his brother's house in Royal Exchange Lane and Maverick at his mother's house in Union Street. They were buried in a common grave. Patrick Carr died a week later and his body was buried in the same tomb on March 17.

III   Trials for Murder

****

1

John Adams Enters the Case

SOME BELLS that rang an alarm at 7 o'clock on the evening of March 5 disturbed John Adams and his club of associates, who were meeting at Henderson Inch's house at the south end of Boston. They snatched up their coats and cloaks and rushed out, expecting to help fight a fire. But there was no fire; instead they learned that there had been shooting. Adams seems to have reached the site when the tumult had died down, and his report is strangely in agreement with certain myopic witnesses who said they saw nothing. At the south door of the Town House he noted some small field pieces and some engineers and grenadiers drawn up to protect them. He feared the alarm might have affected Mrs. Adams, who was alone in the house except for maids and a boy, and who was "in circumstances." Observing that all was quiet around the Town House Adams walked down Boylston Alley into Brattle Square and found a company or two of regular soldiers drawn up in front of Dr. Cooper's old church, "with their muskets all shouldered and their bayonets all fixed. I had no other way to proceed but along the whole front in a very narrow space which they had left for foot passengers. Pursuing my way without taking the least notice of them or they of me, any more than if they had been marble statues, I went directly home to Cold Lane."

On arriving at his house Adams noted that his wife, "having heard that the town was still and likely to continue so, had recovered from her first apprehensions and we had nothing but our reflections to interrupt our repose." These reflections, however, deal so precisely with the possible consequences of the riot, that they suggest Adams had absorbed more details before he entered this passage in his diary. He mentions that for many months there had been systematic endeavors "by certain busy characters to excite quarrels, rencounters and combats, single and compound in the night between the inhabitants of the lower class and the soldiers, and at all risks to enkindle an immortal hatred between them." He thought the explosion that had been planned had now occurred. He then weighed the consequences for the "poor fools" who had become the tools of designing men. "If the soldiers in self-defense should kill any of them, they must be tried, and if truth was respected and the law prevailed, must be acquitted. To depend upon the perversion of law, and the corruption and partiality of juries, would insensibly disgrace the jurisprudence of the country and corrupt the morals of the people. It would be better for the whole people to rise in their majesty and insist on the removal of the army, and take upon themselves the consequences, than to excite such passions between the people and the soldiers, as would expose both to continual prosecution, civil or criminal, and keep the town boiling in a continual fermentation."

This passage in Adams' *Autobiography* was written years after the event it describes, and must be considered an effort at justification of the subsequent activities he engaged in. It also helps explain the attitude John Adams took when he became directly involved in the consequences of the massacre on the following morning. He went to his law office, which was located near the stairs of the Town House, without giving any attention to the locale of the shooting on the night before. He was in his law office when a Boston merchant named James Forrest, known in town as the Irish Infant, entered in a highly agitated state, "with tears streaming from his eyes." He begged Adams to become counsel for Captain Thomas Preston, who had been placed in jail to await action by the grand jury on the charge of murder. "I am come with a very solemn message from a very unfortunate man, Captain Preston, in prison," said Forrest. "He wishes for counsel and can get none. I have waited on Mr. Quincy [Josiah Quincy, Jr.] who says he will engage if you will give him your assistance; without it he positively will not. Even Mr. [Robert] Auchmuty declines, unless you will engage."

Adams knew that the defense of a British officer in a capital case would be deeply resented by his fellow-townsmen, but his detestation of mob action and adherence to principle made him a logical prospect for the defense. Adams' thoughts must have been racing through his head, for he saw this "as important a cause as ever was tried in any court or country of the world," calling for nothing but fact, evidence and law, no art or address.

"Captain Preston requested and desired no more," said

Forrest, and Adams records "that he had such an opinion from all he had heard from all parties of me that he could cheerfully trust his life with me upon those principles." Forrest continued: "As God almighty is my judge I believe him an innocent man."

"That must be ascertained at his trial, and if he thinks he cannot have a fair trial of that issue without my assistance, without hesitation he shall have it."

Forrest pressed a guinea into Adams' hand and left.

Later Hutchinson, who was a historian as well as an administrator, seemed to disclose that Forrest's despair was part of shrewd strategy. Hutchinson said Preston had been advised "to retain two gentlemen of the law who were strongly attached to the cause of liberty, and to stick at no reasonable fee for that purpose."

John Adams expected to be blamed by his fellow townsmen for agreeing to defend the accused soldiers, and there were times when he pretended to be hurt and worried about the effect on his career. Yet before the trials came up the town meeting gave him a resounding vote of confidence by electing him to represent Boston in the lower house of the General Court. Poor James Otis, suffering from periodic mental disability, had resigned and had been succeeded by James Bowdoin. In the general election Bowdoin was chosen a member of the Council, and met with no objection from Acting Governor Hutchinson, who held a veto power. To fill Bowdoin's place as Representative the town meeting nominated Adams and a justice of the peace named Ruddock, who had become wealthy as a master shipwright and was quite popular with tradesmen and mechanics. "Notwithstanding the late clamor

against me," said Adams, "I was chosen by a large majority."

Adams says he had never attended a town meeting up
to this time, which seems extraordinary in view of his interest in public affairs. Now, when messengers brought
him the returns, he went to Faneuil Hall to express his
readiness to serve. But according to the feelings he confided
to his diary, he looked on this assignment as another heavy
burden. He wrote: "I considered the step as a devotion of
my family to ruin, and myself to death; for I could scarce
conceive a possibility that I should ever go through the
thorns and leap all the precipices before me and escape with
my life." This would seem to be a strange attitude for a
man who was doing nothing more dangerous than joining
a legislative assembly, but it is typical of the pessimism
that overtook him when he felt depressed.

He asserted that he now had more legal business than
any man in the Province, but kept telling himself that he
was throwing away as bright prospects as any man ever
faced, and that he had devoted himself to "endless labor
and anxiety, if not to infamy and to death," for nothing
except a sense of duty. He even carried his apprehensions to
his wife, who was burdened with another pregnancy
and household cares, but who knew what to tell John Adams. "That excellent lady, who has always encouraged me,"
wrote Adams in his diary, "burst into a flood of tears, but
said she was very sensible of all the danger to her and to our
children, as well as to me, but she thought I had done as I
ought; she was very willing to share in all that was to come,
and to place her trust in Providence."

Although Boston was aware that John Adams acted

from a high sense of duty, the unknowing, or the malicious, whispering in the taverns, surmised that he had been bought with gold. Adams quickly became aware of the gossip, and his sensitive nature responded. What he wrote in his diary corresponded with what he told Abigail and his intimates. He protested that fees were never mentioned; that he received ten guineas from Preston before the trial and eight more at the trial of the soldiers. He put in fourteen or fifteen days of hard labor on the case, and hazarded popularity, suspicion and prejudice. When he considered the opposition he became cynical: "The memory of malice is faithful, and more, it continually adds to its stock, while that of kindness and friendship is not only frail but treacherous."

2

The Legal Setting

❦

THIRTEEN MEN were indicted for the murder of Boston civilians in King Street on March 5, 1770, and three trials were held during the fall term of the Superior Court of Judicature. The trial of Captain Thomas Preston lasted six days, from October 24 through October 30, with the sabbath intervening, at the end of which he was acquitted. The trial of the eight soldiers of the 24th Regiment began on November 27 and ended on December 5; six men were acquitted and two were found guilty of manslaughter, and upon pleading benefit of clergy, were burned on the left thumb and discharged. More than eighty witnesses were lined up for trials, yet the town committee complained that some of the essential witnesses were not called. The third action on December 12 was perfunctory, and it is puzzling to know why it reached a trial at all. The four men accused of firing guns out of the window of the Custom House had been arrested on the testimony of a French lad whose story was repeated by two men interrogated by the town committee; the evidence was found to be false and the jury acquitted the men without leaving its seats.

This was the most extraordinary judicial proceeding heard in Massachusetts, if not on the continent, during the eighteenth century. Counsel for both the Province and the defense, devoted to the attainment of justice, looked beyond the courtroom to the effect of the verdict on the tense relations between Britain and America. If the prosecution obtained a verdict of murder in the first degree, the soldiers would be sentenced to hang, and the consequences to the Province would be incalculable. The defense attorneys, in trying to get the soldiers off, would have to admit testimony on the bad behavior of the townsmen, and thus have to face the anger of their compatriots. It required all the high purpose and legal adroitness of John Adams to end the controversy without rancor.

Jonathan Sewall, the Attorney General, who drew up the indictments, left Boston immediately after and did not take part in the trials. The selectmen of Boston asked Robert Treat Paine to serve as special prosecutor. Paine was not one of the noisy patriots, but his sympathies no less were with the liberals. In time he was to write his name large on the Declaration of Independence, and to serve as Governor of Massachusetts. He was 39 years old, had attended Harvard and studied theology, and served as chaplain with New England troops in 1758. With a fine prospect of proving the guilt of the soldiers, he conducted his case with such circumspection that he seemed anxious to avoid a conviction. His associate, Samuel Quincy, elder brother of Josiah Quincy, Jr., was a Tory in his views and a lawyer of no great effectiveness.

Counsel for the defense were John Adams and Josiah Quincy, Jr., with Simpson S. Blowers assisting. Robert Auchmuty, Judge of the Vice Admiralty, joined in the defense of Preston. Four years before Adams had recorded his distaste of Auchmuty's courtroom manner, mentioning "the same dull, heavy, insipid way of arguing everywhere; as many repetitions as a Presbyterian parson in his prayer. Volubility, voluble repetition, and repeated volubility; fluent reiterations and reiterating fluency. Such nauseous eloquence always puts my patience to the torture."

Josiah Quincy, Jr., was 26 years old and only seven years out of Harvard College; he had studied law with Oxenbridge Thacher and shared the latter's opposition to British fiscal policies. His defense of the soldiers shocked his father, who wrote him: "It has filled the bosom of your aged and infirm parent with anxiety and distress lest it should not only prove true but destructive of your reputation and interest." But the son's devotion to the cause of liberty was never in doubt, for he was one of the principal orators of the day, outspoken and vehement in debate. Yet Adams and Josiah Quincy were linked together to defend men they considered culpable to a degree, if not of murder at least of manslaughter. In their eyes loomed the larger issue of damage to the patriotic cause if the men did not get a fair trial.

The justices of the Superior Court were Benjamin Lynde, Second Chief Justice, who presided; John Cushing, Peter Oliver, and Edmund Trowbridge. Each had served in various judicial capacities. Trowbridge had been Attorney General. Hutchinson had given up the post of Chief Justice when Governor Bernard left for England in 1769, which made him Acting Governor. John Cushing was the son of a justice and had a son who would eventually become Chief Justice.

No army would try enlisted men and an officer at the same court martial, and neither would the civil courts of Massachusetts. But the eight British soldiers who languished in the inhospitable Boston jail during the hot summer months of 1770 hoped otherwise. When the trial of Captain Preston was announced for October 24 the accused soldiers on October 21 addressed a fervent appeal to the Court from the jail:

"We poor distressed prisoners beg that ye would be so good as to let us have our trial at the same time with our Captain, for we did our Captain's orders, and if we do not obey his command should have been confined and shot for not doing it. We only desire to open the truths before our Captain's face for it is very hard [that] he, being a gentle-man, should have more chance for to save his life when [than] we poor men that is obliged to obey his command."

The appeal was signed by Hugh White, James Hartegan, and Matthew Killroy, the latter making his mark (x). The Court denied it.

The indictment drawn against Captain Preston and the British soldiers, on which they were tried, is a document of such formidable verbiage that its text is usually omitted by historians. Its repetitious phraseology is an example, however, of how legal practice attempted to close all loop-holes and make the charge specific and unassailable. Readers today may find that it taxes their patience, but it should interest them as a document typical of the sort the lawyers of 18th century Boston encountered almost daily. Nor has modern practice made many improvements on it. It also is of special interest because it becomes explicit in describing the wounds of one of the victims—Crispus Attucks. Here it is:

> At His Majesty's Superior Court of Judicature, Court of Assizes, and General Gaol Delivery, begun and held at Boston within and for the County of Suffolk, on the second Tuesday of March, in the tenth reign of George the Third, by the grace of God, of Great Britain, France and Ireland King, Defender of the Faith, &c.
>
> The jurors for the said Lord the King, upon their oath present, that Thomas Preston, Esq., William Weems, laborer, James Hartegan, laborer, William McCauley, laborer, Hugh White, laborer, Matthew Killroy, laborer, William Warren, laborer, John Carroll, laborer, and Hugh Montgomery, laborer, all now resident in Boston, in the County of Suffolk, and Hammond Green, boat builder, Thomas Greenwood, laborer, Edward Manwaring, Esq., and John Munroe, gentleman, all of Boston aforesaid, not having the fear of God before their eyes, but being moved and seduced by the instigation of the devil and their own wicked hearts, did, on the fifth day of March, at Boston, with force of arms, feloniously, willfully, and of their malice aforethought, assault one Crispus Attucks, then and there being in the peace of God, and of the said Lord the King, and that he, the said William Warren, with a certain hand gun of the value of twenty shillings, which he, the said William Warren, then and there held in both his hands, charged with gunpowder and two leaden bullets, then and there, feloniously, willfully, and of his malice aforethought. did shoot off, and discharge at and against the said Crispus Attucks, and that the said William Warren, with the leaden bullets as aforesaid, out of the said hand gun, then and there, by force of the said gun powder so shot off and discharged as aforesaid, did then and there, feloniously, willfully, and by his malice aforethought, strike, penetrate, and wound the said Cris-

pus Attucks in and upon the right breast, a little below the right pap of him the said Crispus, and in and upon the left breast, a little below the left pap of him, the said Crispus, thereby giving to him, the said Crispus, with one of the bullets aforesaid, so shot off and discharged as aforesaid, in and upon the right breast, a little below the right pap of him, the said Crispus, one mortal wound of the depth of six inches, and of the width of one inch; and also giving to him, the said Crispus, with the other bullet aforesaid, so shot off and discharged by the said William Warren as aforesaid, in and upon the left breast, a little below the left pap of him, the said Crispus, one mortal wound of the depth of six inches, and of the width of one inch, of which said mortal wounds, the said Crispus Attucks then and there instantly died; and that the aforesaid Thomas Preston, William Weems, James Hartegan, William McCauley, Hugh White, Matthew Killroy, William Warren, John Carroll, Hugh Montgomery, Hammond Green, Thomas Greenwood, Edward Manwaring, and John Munroe, then and there, feloniously, willfully, and of their malice aforethought, were present, aiding, helping, abetting, comforting, assisting, and maintaining the said William Warren, to do and commit the felony and murder aforesaid.

And so the jurors aforesaid, upon their said oath, do say that the Thomas Preston [*repeating the names of the accused*] did kill and murder the said Crispus Attucks, against the peace of the said Lord the King, his crown and dignity.

JOHN SEWALL, Atty. pro Dom. Rege. WILLIAM TAYLOR, Foreman.

This true bill places the responsibility for the death of only one victim on William Warren specifically, and on the other accused men generally. It was necessary to return similar true bills against the soldiers who had shot the four other victims. Samuel Winthrop, clerk, attests that James

Hartegan was indicted for the murder of Samuel Gray, Matthew Killroy for that of Samuel Maverick, John Carroll for that of James Caldwell, and Hugh White for that of Patrick Carr. The testimony, however, differs from these allocations.

3

The Responsibility of Captain Preston

CAPTAIN THOMAS PRESTON was the first of the accused to be placed on trial. As stated above the trial lasted six days, with the sabbath intervening, from October 24 through October 30, 1770. He was acquitted. The jury deliberated only a few hours, but because Robert Treat Paine was unable to finish his closing address to the jury on Saturday, court was held over to the following Monday. This meant the jurors had to be kept confined over Sunday, but the court gave them "liberty of the court house" with their keepers.

No transcript of the trial is available. John Adams said the trial was taken down in shorthand by John Hodgson and "transmitted to England without any known authority but his own. The British Government have never permitted it to see the light, and probably never will." A concept of the sort of evidence presented can be obtained from the testimony of some of the eighty witnesses who were lined up for the second trial of the eight private soldiers, and from references made by those who had some knowledge of the proceedings.

Before considering the trial itself it is necessary to refer again to the preliminary examination of Captain Preston conducted by Justices Dania and Tudor in the early morning hours after the massacre of March 5, and to certain publications by him while he was in jail waiting to be tried. The original investigation concentrated on whether or not Preston had given the soldiers an order to fire on the mob, and this turned out to be the pivotal issue when he came up for trial. After the shooting Captain Preston looked after the disposition of the troops with the object of countering further trouble in the streets and then surrendered to the Sheriff. Judge John Tudor wrote in his diary: "The Captain commanded the soldiers to fire." He also wrote: "Captain Preston was taken up by a warrant given to the High Sheriff by Justices Dania and Tudor and came under examination about 2 o'clock, and we sent him to gaol soon after 3, having evidence sufficient to commit him on his ordering the soldiers to fire." Captain Preston's contention, from the very start, was that he did not order the soldiers to fire.

In Boston Gaol Captain Preston was seized with panic. Officials and sympathizers who commisserated with him heard his fervent appeals for getting him out of his difficult situation. He even sent a letter to the publishers of the *Boston Gazette*, which they published in the issue that contained an account of the King Street tragedy. It read:

> Messrs. Edes & Gill: Permit me thro' the channel of your paper, to return my thanks in the most public manner to the inhabitants in general of this town—who throwing aside all party and prejudice, have with the utmost

humanity and freedom stept forth advocates for truth, in defense of my injured innocence, in this late unhappy affair that happened on Monday night last: and to assure them that I shall ever have the highest sense of the justice they have done me, which will be ever gratefully remembered by

Their much obliged and most obedient humble servant,
THOMAS PRESTON

After thus trying to find favor with the people of Boston, Captain Preston turned to persuade the Britons at home that he was not to blame for the tragedy. He must have begun his defense at once, for John Robinson, the Commissioner of Customs, carried it when he embarked for London a week later and it was published in the *Public Advertiser* there on April 28.

It took eight weeks for Captain Preston's London letter to reach Boston, but the delay did not weaken the impact. Extraordinary editions—today's "extras"—appeared. The *Massachusetts Gazette Extraordinary* was published on June 21; the *Boston Gazette* and the *Boston Evening Post* issued supplements with the letter on June 25. The contents stirred up more animosity against the Captain. His statement opened with a denunciation of the tactics of the Bostonians, whom he accused of abusive behavior toward the soldiers. "They have ever used all means in their power to weaken the regiments and to bring them into contempt, by promoting and aiding desertions, and by grossly and falsely propagating untruths concerning them." He described the fracas at Gray's Ropewalk and said "this violence and the utter hatred of the troops increased daily."

He then made several accusations that caused more anger among the patriots. He said five or six leaders had

agreed privately on a general engagement, "in conse-
quence of which several of the militia came from the country, armed to join their friends, menacing to destroy any
who should oppose them." He said men broke into two
meeting houses to ring the bells that were a signal to attack the troops. The mob then went to the Custom
House, "where the King's money is lodged, with clubs and
other weapons to execute their revenge on the sentinel."
Preston asserted he was told they probably would murder the sentinel as a "prelude to plundering the King's
chest."

Captain Preston said he sent a non-com and twelve (*sic*)
men to protect the sentinel and the King's money, and followed; that the men went with unloaded pieces, and he
gave no order for loading them. He was in front of the soldiers and was hit on the arm by a club.

"On my asking the soldiers why they fired without orders they said they heard the word *fire* and supposed it came
from me. This might be the case as many of the mob
called out 'Fire!' 'Fire!', but I assured the men, that I
gave no such order and that my words were 'Don't
fire; stop your firing!' On the people assembling to take
away the dead bodies the soldiers, supposing them coming to attack again, were ready to fire again, which I pre-
vented by striking up their firelocks with my hand."

He sent the party and the sentry to the main guard,
"telling them off into streeet firings, divided and planted
them at each end of the street to secure their rear, momen-
tarily expecting an attack, as there was a constant cry of
the inhabitants: 'To arms!' 'To arms!' 'Turn out with your
guns,' and the town drums beating to arms. I ordered my
drum to beat to arms, and being soon after joined by the

different companies of the 29th Regiment, I formed them as the guard into street firing. The 14th Regiment also got under arms but remained at their barracks.

"I immediately sent a party to Colonel Dalrymple to acquaint him with every particular. Several officers going to their regiments were knocked down by the mob; one very much wounded and his sword taken from him. The Lieutenant Governor and Colonel Carr soon after met at the head of the 29th Regiment and agreed that the regiment should retire to their barracks, and the people to their houses, but I kept the piquet [picket] to strengthen the guard. It was with great difficulty that the Lieutenant Governor prevailed on the people to be quiet and retire. At last they all went off except about a hundred."

Preston described the calling of the Council, the arrest of himself and the eight soldiers, and the interrogation by Justices Dania and Tudor. He said he could have escaped easily, had he had any feeling of guilt. He accused the witnesses of confusion and misrepresentation. Two witnesses testified that Preston gave the order to fire, one saying he swore at the men for not firing at the first word. Others swore they heard Preston use the word *fire*. "So bitter and inveterate are many of the malcontents here," wrote Preston, "that they are industriously using every method to fish out evidence to prove it was a concerted scheme to murder the inhabitants. Others are infusing the utmost malice and revenge into the minds of the people who are to be my jurors, by false publications, votes of towns, and all other artifices, (to form?) a settled rancour against the officers and troops in general—the suddenness of my trial after the affair, while the people's minds are greatly inflamed. I am though perfectly innocent, under most unhappy circumstances, having nothing in reason to expect but the loss of life in a very ignominious manner, without the interposition of his majesty's royal goodness."

The effect of this defense by Preston was catastrophic; all the pent up anger at the redcoats burst forth in public addresses, newspaper editorials, and indignation meetings. The accusations that caused the most feeling were, that there had been some private understanding to murder the soldiers, and that the mob had intended to kill the sentry and rob the "King's chest."

Preston was then in jail, awaiting trial. Samuel Adams confronted him with the article and asked whether he was the author. Preston admitted he had "drawn a state of his case, but it had passed through different hands and was altered at different times." Adams then asked whether the parts to which he took exception were Preston's own writings or by other hands. This Preston refused to clarify, explaining that if he did he might displease friends who had acted in good faith and whose help he might need.

This subterfuge Adams could not accept. When the Town of Boston later appointed him one of a committee of nine to prepare "a true state of the Town and the acts of the commissioners" he carefully described this interview in their report to Benjamin Franklin, then in London. He added:

"So shocked was Captain Preston himself at its [the article's] appearance in the light on this side of the water that he was immediately apprehensive. So glaring a falsehood would raise the indignation of the people to such a pitch as to prompt them to some attempts that would be dangerous to him, and he accordingly applied to Mr. Sheriff Greenleaf for special protection on that account; but the Sheriff assuring him that there was no such disposition appearing among the people (which is an undoubted truth) Captain Preston's fears at length subsided, and he still remains in safe custody."

Captain Preston may have conveyed a feeling of helplessness in what he wrote, but he was not ready to face his accusers without a fight. He had three courses open to him. One was to get the best liberal lawyers in town. This tactic was suggested by his friends and it succeeded to the great satisfaction of Thomas Hutchinson. When the Irish merchant James Forrest wept tears over the hard lot of Preston in John Adams' office he snared both Adams and young Quincy for the defense. The second move was to line up witnesses who would exonerate the Captain of any blame. Since a transcript is not available we must draw inferences from the testimony at the trial of the soldiers. None of the witnesses was quite positive that Preston gave an order to fire, and some, who may or may not have been suborned, were certain he did not give one. The third maneuver was the time-honored method of packing the jury panel. In this his friends succeeded admirably, and no doubt helped bring about his quick acquittal.

Did Captain Preston order the soldiers to fire? Lieutenant Governor Hutchinson evidently had asked how he happened to fire without an order from a magistrate, but Preston's answer was lost in the turmoil. Samuel Adams, after the trial, belabored this point; he wrote the *Boston Gazette*: "The Chief Magistrate asked the officer who commanded: 'Did you not know that you should not have fired without the order of a civil magistrate?' It is sworn that Preston answered: 'I did it to save my sentry.'" Presum-

ably this evidence was given at the preliminary interrogation, which Preston disputed. He said two men swore
he gave the order to fire, one that he stood within two
feet of him; "the other that I swore at the men for not
firing at the first word. Others swore they heard me use
the word fire, but whether do or do not fire they could
not say; others that they heard the word fire but could not
say it came from me."

There is also a record that at the trial Captain Preston
asked Captain James Gifford: "Did you ever know an
officer [to] order men to fire with their bayonets charged?"
Gifford replied: "No."

The strongest argument supporting Preston's assertion of innocence is the action of the soldiers themselves.
According to testimony in the second trial, and reiterated
by others, the first shot was fired by Montgomery after he
had his gun knocked out of his hands; he retrieved it and
fired point blank. The other shots followed erratically, and
one gun flashed in the pan. There was no volley such as
would have followed an order.

This subject of civilian control over the actions of the
military was raised by Justice Trowbridge in his summing
up, presumbly at the second trial. It is placed here because of its pertinence to the situation of Captain Preston:

"It seems a doctrine has of late been advanced 'that soldiers while on duty may upon *no occasion whatever* fire
upon their fellow subjects without the order of a civil magistrate.' This may possibly account for some of those who
attacked the soldiers, saying to them: 'You dare not fire;
we know you dare not fire.' But it ought to be known
that the law doth not countenance such an absurd doctrine.

A man by becoming a soldier doth not thereby lose the right of self-defense, which is provided in the law of nature. Where any one is, without his own default, reduced to such circumstances as that the laws of society cannot avail him, the law considers him *as still in that instance* under the protection of the law of nature."

Preston's statement that the soldiers' guns were not loaded was contradicted by Samuel Adams, who wrote that they arrived with loaded guns and fixed bayonets. Josiah Simpson, however, testified that the officer gave the command "prime and load." Benjamin Lee said the sentry loaded his gun after he had knocked at the door of the Custom House.

Lieut. Colonel Carr had confidence in the integrity of Preston. He said Preston was known to be "as cool and distinct" an officer as any of his rank in the service. He was confident Preston did not give the order to fire. Lieut. Colonel Dalrymple asserted the crowd had tried to make a "considerable disturbance" in order to get the troops removed.

A few weeks before Preston's trial opened Lord Hillsborough apprised General Gage of the King's pleasure to have him supply Preston with such sums as he needed for defense, and to charge this to military contingencies. "Lord North and I, upon a consideration of this matter, are of the opinion that this service ought not to appear on a public account. The King therefore takes the expense upon himself . . . We suppose this expense cannot exceed a few hundreds (of pounds)."

Captain Preston was acquitted of the charge of murder, the jury deliberating only a few hours although remaining together overnight. The outcome was most satisfying to the administration. Acting Governor Hutchinson, in a letter found later, wrote Governor Bernard, who had gone to England, that he was pleased with Captain Joseph Mayo of Roxbury, who was foreman of the jury. "I am much inclined to make him a major," said Hutchinson. He advanced him to major of the First Suffolk Regiment. Mayo, however, had a good record as a patriot.

Samuel Adams was highly critical of the acquittal of Captain Preston. He declared that not only was damaging testimony disregarded, but that a number of the jurors were biased. He said the baker of the regiment, who would have preferred to be excused, and three other doubtful persons, were put on as talesmen, after Preston's counsel had challenged nineteen. One was a known intimate of Preston, according to Adams, and another had said that if he were chosen a member of the jury he could sit until doomsday before agreeing to a verdict against Preston. The clerk of the court noted that Preston peremptorily challenged nineteen—fifteen of the county jurors and four talesmen, as well as two others of the county, which were not considered peremptory because he did not have their names before the trial.

Adams was well justified when he asserted that Preston's jury contained friends who would acquit him. In the *Legal Papers of John Adams*, and in the American Bar Association *Journal* for April, 1969, Professors Hiller B. Zobel and L. Kivin Wroth name five jurors, who later became loyalist exiles, who were known as supporters of Preston. The conclusive proof of the culpability of one of them, a Boston merchant named Gilbert Deblois, was found in the Audit Office records of the Public Record Office, London. The authors discovered that in the 1780s Thomas Preston testified in an action by Deblois to get compensation for war losses from a London board. Preston said Deblois investigated the character of many of the persons returned for jurors, which enabled Preston to set aside most of those returned by the town, who were radicals, and pick some of the moderates who came from the county. Deblois also won a place on the panel, stayed in the jail with the other jurors during Preston's trial, detected evidences of perjury, and by his personal influence was "a great means" of getting Preston acquitted.

When Captain Preston was freed his relief was unbounded. His volatile nature expressed itself in letters to General Gage. He wrote: "I take the liberty of wishing you joy at the complete victory obtained over the knaves and foolish villains of Boston; the triumph is now almost complete and the King's servants now appear with double luster."

He also took the occasion to comment on his defense. "The counsel for the Crown, or rather the town, were poor and managed badly; my counsel on the contrary were men of parts and exerted themselves with great spirit and cleverness, particularly Judge Auchmuty. The judges also were determined and showed much firmness, but none more than Judge Oliver; he informed the court that he had been abused in some prints and his life threatened, but that nothing should daunt him or prevent his doing his duty."

Judge Robert Auchmuty sided with the British in the Revolution. Judge Oliver was a brother of Andrew Oliver, Secretary of State for the Province and a brother-in-law of Acting Governor Hutchinson. Preston certainly was loyal to his party. "I thought a saving on a lawyer's fee very impolitick," he said.

A new hazard now threatened him. He had escaped being held accountable for the killings, but there was fear he might be subjected to damage suits from the families of the dead and wounded. Whether suits had validity after his acquittal was questionable, but they might lead to Preston's detention for a long time. He applied quickly for quarters in the barracks at Castle William, outside the jurisdiction of the court, and for passage home. Until his vessel sailed on December 10 he did not set foot again in Boston. England salved his hurts by giving him a pension of 200 pounds.

4

The Trial of the Soldiers

❧

MORE THAN three weeks elapsed between the end of Captain Preston's trial on October 30 and the beginning of the trial of the eight soldiers of the 24th Regiment on November 27, 1770. It was heard by the justices who had presided at Preston's trial. Robert Treat Paine and Samuel Quincy represented the prosecution, Judge Robert Auchmuty having withdrawn. John Adams and Josiah Quincy, Jr., conducted the defense.

The transcript of this trial was made by Thomas Hodgson and published by J. Fleeming in Boston in 1770. The edition usually available was printed in 1824. It purports to contain the depositions that had been collected. There are also partial reports of the summaries by two justices, Oliver and Trowbridge. There is the likelihood that the stenographer wrote up his notes after each session, for the continuity of the evidence is often broken.

Never before had so many witnesses been called to testify at a trial in the Province. Few proceedings, it was said, lasted overnight. When the court was faced with the prospect of days and perhaps weeks of sessions it decided that the jurors must be protected from contact with what Boston called "the inhabitants." This precaution was taken before Preston's trial. The jurors would have to be locked up, provided with sleeping quarters, and served meals at the expense of the Province. The sheriff was duly disturbed. He had to accommodate up to sixteen persons daily, for besides the jurors there was the officer of the Court, one man chosen by the King's attorneys, and one by defense counsel. The sheriff's itemized bill is extant and indicates that the men were supplied with little more than "biscett and cheese and syder" for meals, accompanied by "sperites licker." The foreman of the jury was Captain Joseph Mayo of Roxbury.

Upon being arraigned each prisoner was asked to plead. Each man replied: "Not guilty."

"How wilt thou be tried?"

"By God and my country."

"God send thee a good deliverance."

Samuel Quincy was reserved in his opening address to the jury, and this tone prevailed during most of the trial. He explained: "The cause is solemn and profound; no less than whether eight of your fellow subjects shall live or die. A cause grounded on the most melancholy event that has yet taken place on the continent of America, and perhaps of the greatest expectation of any that has yet come before a tribunal of civil justice, in this part of the British dominions. . . . However interesting the question may be, the object of our inquiry is simply that of truth."

The defense had engaged in a difficult task; it had to get the soldiers freed of the charge of murder, and at the same time avoid making the people of Boston wholly responsible for the violence. Josiah Quincy began this maneuver by impressing on the jurors that there must be no identification of the people of the town with the "rude behavior of a mixed and ungovernable multitude." His argument was that "Boston and its inhabitants have no more to do with this cause than you or any other members of the community. You are, therefore, by no means to blend two things, so eventually different, as the guilt or innocence of this town and the prisoners together. The inhabitants of Boston, by no rule of law, justice or common sense, can be supposed answerable for the unjustifiable conduct of a few individuals hastily assembled in the streets."

This was quite in order, until the witnesses began describing how they happened to go from their homes to the gathering in King Street, some of them carrying sticks and swords. Quincy pressed some of them hard to make them appear full of evil intent, to such a point that John Adams became alarmed. He had to draw Quincy aside and warn him that he was becoming too vehement. It is sometimes said that he had to threaten to leave the case unless Quincy modified his methods, but evidence for this statement is lacking.

The hard lot of the soldier in an inhospitable town was described by Quincy in a moving appeal to the feelings of the jurors:

"Instead of that hospitality that the soldier thought himself entitled to, scorn, contempt, and silent murmurs were his reception. Almost every countenance lowered with a discontented gloom, and scarce an eye but flashed with indignant fire. How stinging was it to be stigmatized as the instrument of tyranny and oppression! How exasperating to be viewed as aiding to enthrall his country! Could that spirit which had braved the shafts of foreign battle endure the keener wounds of civic battle?"

Quincy referred to Paul Revere's engraving of the Boston Massacre as prejudicial: "The prints exhibited in our houses have added wings to fancy, and in the fervor of our zeal, reason is in hazard of being lost."

The events of the evening of March 5, 1770, in Boston, were seen by hundreds of people. Many were asked to tell what they saw, by the news reporters and the counsel for and against the soldiers. The basic facts are not a matter of dispute, but the details vary. Despite the repetition, the accounts admirably reflect the temper of the hour, the attitudes of the spectators, and their personal bias.

There was disagreement among the witnesses about the size of the mob. Some saw twenty men, others fifty to 100; one man counted only twelve facing the soldiers. There was continuing movement, new spectators coming in from Cornhill. None, apparently, heeded the admonitions of older heads telling the crowd to go home. Although some witnesses said they saw nothing thrown at the soldiers, the preponderance of evidence was that not only were pieces of ice and chunks of coal thrown, but the soldiers were menaced and struck on the guns with sticks.

Ebenezer Bridgham saw many things thrown, but could not say what they were.

"How did the soldiers stand?"

"They stood with their pieces before them, to defend themselves, and as soon as they had placed themselves a party, about twelve in number, with sticks in their hands, who stood in the middle of the street, gave three cheers, and immediately surrounded the soldiers, and struck upon their guns with their sticks, and passed along the front of the soldiers, towards Royal Exchange Lane, striking the soldiers' guns as they passed."

"Did you apprehend the soldiers in danger, from anything you saw?"

"I did not, indeed. I saw the people near me on the left strike the soldiers' guns, daring them to fire, and called them cowards and rascals for bringing arms against naked men; bid them lay aside their guns, and they were their men."

Asked whether the men around the soldiers were sailors or townsmen, Bridgham replied some of them were dressed in the habits of sailors.

Richard Palmes, who had admonished the officer at Murray's Barracks earlier in the evening, was interested in seeing order kept. When he reached the Town House and heard a disturbance he learned there was a "rumpus" at the Custom House. He said to a man named Spear: "I will go down and make peace." Spear said: "You had better not go." But Palmes disagreed and went down and saw Captain Preston at the head of seven or eight soldiers with fixed bayonets. He heard Theodore Bliss say to Preston: "Why do you not fire? God damn you, fire!"

"I slipped between them," said Palmes, "and asked Captain Preston if the soldiers were loaded. He said: 'Yes, with powder and ball.' I said: 'Sir, I hope you are not going to fire on the inhabitants.' He said: 'By no means.'

"That instant I saw a piece of ice strike Montgomery's gun; whether it sallied him back or he stepped one foot back I do not know, but he recovered himself and fired immediately. I thought he stepped back and fired; he was the next man to Captain Preston that was betwixt the Captain and the Custom House. When he fired I heard the word *fire;* who gave it I do not know. Six or eight seconds after that another soldier on the Captain's right fired, and then the rest, one after another, pretty quick, then there was an interval of two or three seconds between the last gun but one, and the last."

Palmes now got into a tussle with Montgomery. Before the last gun was fired Montgomery made a lunge at him with his bayonet. "I had a stick in my hand, as I generally walk with one," said Palmes; "I struck him and hit his left arm, and knocked his gun down; before he recovered I aimed another stroke at the nearest (man) to him and hit Captain Preston. I saw Montgomery pushing at me again and would have pushed me through, but I threw my stick in his face. The third time he ran after me to put at me again but fell down, and I had an opportunity to run down Royal Exchange Lane."

James Bailey disagreed with Palmes on the sequence of events. He contended that Montgomery was knocked down before he fired. This seems to have been the impression of others, and is quite plausible, for the firing precipitated a crisis and there was hardly any scuffling after that. When Palmes was questioned further he contributed a bit of unintentional humor:

"Upon the firing of the first gun, did the people seem to retire?"

"Yes, they all began to run, and when the rest were firing they were all a-running."

"When the last gun was fired, where were the people?"

"They were running promiscuously about everywhere."

While some of the spectators were not always sure of

what they heard and saw, Edward G. Langford, a member of the Town Watch, was precise in his statement that he saw Matthew Killroy shoot Samuel Gray before his eyes. He barely escaped injury from Killroy's bayonet. When the bell started ringing Langford suspected more trouble at Murray's Barracks and rushed out, then found that the disturbance there had ended. Approaching the Town Pump he saw twenty to twentyfive boys going into King Street, and then found a group around the sentry box at the Custom House. The crowd had crossed the gutter, which meant that it stood close to the steps of the Custom House. He asked what the trouble was and was told the sentry had knocked down a boy. Langford, acting with his customary authority, told the men to let the sentry alone; then he went up the steps of the Custom House and knocked on the door, but got no response. He told the sentry not to be afraid; these were only boys and would not hurt him. Soon after, the sentry walked up the steps and called for help. When he stepped down he levelled his gun at the crowd, with his bayonet fixed.

Langford stood there when the file of soldiers arrived and heard someone, probably Palmes, say: "Are you loaded?" He heard no orders to load. Samuel Gray, the ropewalk employee, stepped up to Langford, struck him on the shoulder, and said: "Langford, what's here to pay?"

"I said I did not know what was to pay, but I believed something would come of it by and by. He made no reply."

Langford was standing close to the soldiers, within reach of their bayonets, and Killroy was in front of him. Two guns went off. "I looked this man in the face and bid him not fire—I said either 'damn you, or God damn you, do not fire,' but he fired immediately, and Samuel Gray fell at my feet." Gray had thrown no snowballs, had no weapon, and had said nothing to the soldiers; his hands were in his bosom as he fell, said Langford. Then Killroy thrust his bayonet through Langford's jacket and greatcoat.

One of the most natural accounts of the massacre was related by a Negro manservant, a witness for the defense, who is identified in the record only as Andrew. He told his story at the trial of the soldiers more than seven months after the shooting in King Street. The narrative is circumstantial and convincing, and although the scribe undoubtedly eliminated many individual touches, it has the quality of folklore.

Andrew opened his testimony by telling that a friend had told him that a soldier with a cutlass had struck him on the arm and "almost cut it off." "I said a good club was better than a cutlass and he had better go down and see if he could not cut some too."

The boys were throwing snowballs. Andrew saw that the sentinels (soldiers) were enraged and swearing at the boys. The boys were calling out: "lobsters," "bloody backs," and yelling: "Who buys lobsters?"

Andrew heard three cheers given in King Street. He went down to the whipping post and stood by Waldo's shop. People standing near him were picking up pieces of sea coal and snowballs and throwing them at the sentry.

"While I was standing there the boys cried out: 'We have got his gun away and now we will have him.' Presently I heard cheers given by the people at the Custom House."

What the cheering was for Andrew did not say, but just about then the soldiers arrived. "I saw a file of men, with an officer with a laced hat on, before them." At the head of Royal Exchange Lane he heard a grenadier say to a man who stood beside him: "Damn you, stand back!"

Andrew was so near that the grenadier might have run him through if he had taken one step forward. A man came between the grenadier and Andrew and the soldier "had like to have pricked him; he turned about and said: 'You damned lobster, bloody back, you are going to stab me'; the soldier said 'by God, I will.'

"Presently somebody took hold of me by the shoulder and told me to go home, or I should be hurt; at the same time there were a number of people towards the Town Hall who said: "Come away and let the guard alone, you have nothing at all to do with them.' "

Andrew now saw that some of the people were talking with the officer, who was standing in front of the soldiers. A number were jumping on the backs of those that were talking with the officer in order to get as near as they could.

"One of the persons that was talking with the officer turned about quick to the people and said: 'Damn him, he is going to fire.' Upon that they gave a great shout and cried out: 'Fire and be damned; who cares for you, you dare not fire.' And began to throw snowballs and other things, which then flew very thick."

"Did they hit any of them?"

"Yes, I saw two or three of them hit; one struck a grenadier on the hat, and the people who were right behind them had sticks, and as the soldiers were pushing with their guns back and forth they struck their guns, and one hit a grenadier on the fingers. At this time the people up at the Town House called again, 'Come away! Come away!' A

The BLOODY MASSACRE perpetrated in King—:Street BOSTON on March 5th 1770, by a party of the 29th REGT.

Engrav'd Printed & Sold by PAUL REVERE BOSTON.

BUTCHER'S HALL

Unhappy BOSTON! see thy Sons deplore,
Thy hallow'd Walks besmear'd with guiltless Gore.
While faithless P——n and his savage Bands,
With murd'rous Rancour stretch their bloody Hands;
Like fierce Barbarians grinning o'er their Prey,
Approve the Carnage, and enjoy the Day.

If scalding drops from Rage from Anguish Wrung,
If speechless Sorrows lab'ring for a Tongue,
Or if a weeping World can ought appease
The plaintive Ghosts of Victims such as these;
The Patriot's copious Tears for each are shed,
A glorious Tribute which embalms the Dead.

But know Fate summons to that awful Goal,
Where Justice strips the Murd'rer of his Soul:
Should venal C——ts the scandal of the Land,
Snatch the relentless Villain from her Hand,
Keen Execrations on this Plate inscrib'd,
Shall reach a JUDGE who never can be brib'd.

The unhappy Sufferers were Mess.rs SAM.L GRAY, SAM.L MAVERICK, JAM.S CALDWELL, CRISPUS ATTUCKS & PAT.K CARR
Killed. Six wounded; two of them (CHRIST.R MONK & JOHN CLARK) Mortally

Paul Revere's Engraving of the Boston Massacre   *New York Public Library*

Old State House, Facing the Former King Street, Where the Massacre Occurred
Samuel Chamberlain Photo

Washington Street Front of Old State House. From an Improvised Balcony
Above the Door Washington Reviewed His Victorious Troops

Samuel Chamberlain Photo

Samuel Adams, Agitator for Freedom from British Taxation
New York Public Library

John Adams, Defender of the British Soldiers and Boston's Reputation
New York Public Library

Council Chamber in the Old State House, Boston   *Samuel Chamberlain Photo*

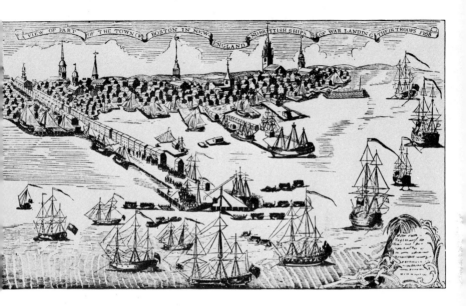

Landing of the British Troops in Boston, 1768. Sketch from Paul Revere's
Engraving   *New York Public Library*

The Old Granary Burying Ground, Where the Victims of the Boston Massacre
Are Buried   *Samuel Chamberlain Photo*

Paul Revere. Portrait by John Singleton Copley. 1738-1815.

Courtesy, Museum of Fine Arts, Boston

Colonial Bedroom and Kitchen in the Paul Revere House

Restored Paul Revere House, Boston   *Samuel Chamberlain Photos*

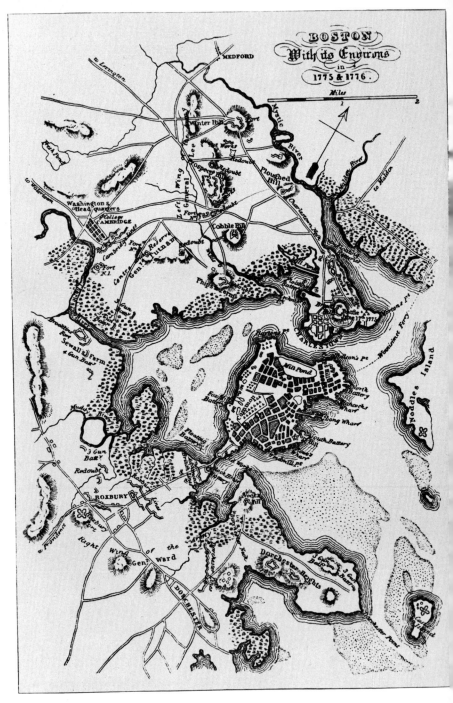

Boston and Environs in 1775 and 1776. From an Old Map *New York Public Libra*

stout man who stood near me and right before the grenadiers, as they pushed with their bayonets with the length
of their arms, kept striking on their guns."

Here Andrew, or possibly the stenographer, dropped
this line of narrative to tell of an interruption. The people
seemed to him to be leaving the soldiers and turning from
them when a new group came from Jackson's Corner,
"huzzaing and crying 'Damn them, they dare not fire, we
are not afraid of them.' " Then he got to the heart of the
fracas:

"One of the people, a stout man with a long cordwood
stick, threw himself in and made a blow at the officer. I
saw the officer try to ward off the stroke, whether he
struck him or not I do not know. The stout man then
turned round and struck the grenadier's gun at the Captain's right hand and immediately fell in with his club
and knocked his gun away, and struck him over the head—
the blow came either on the soldier's cheek or hat. This
stout man held the bayonet with his left hand and twitched
it and cried: 'Kill the dogs, knock them over!'; this was
the general cry. The people then crowded in, and upon
that the grenadier gave a twitch back and relieved his gun
and he up with it and began to pay away on the people. I
was then betwixt the officer and this grenadier. I turned to
go off when I heard the word *fire*. At that word I thought
I heard the report of a gun, and upon my hearing the report I saw the same grenadier swing his gun and immediately he discharged it."

"Do you know who this stout man was that fell in and
struck the grenadier?"

"I thought and still think it was the mulatto who was
shot."

"Do you know the grenadier who was thus assaulted, and fired?"

"I think that it was Killroy, and I told Mr. Quincy so the next morning. I now think it was he from my best observation, but I can't possibly swear it."

"Did the soldiers of that party, or any of them, step or move out of the rank in which they stood, to push the people?"

"No, and if they had they might have killed me and many others with their bayonets."

"Did you, as you passed through the people towards Royal Exchange Lane and the party, see a number of people take up any and every thing they could find in the street and throw them at the soldiers?"

"Yes, I saw ten or fifteen round me do that."

"Did you yourself pick up every thing you could find and throw at them?"

"Yes, I did."

"After the gun fired where did you go?"

"I run as fast as I could into the first door I saw open, which I think was Mr. Dehon's. I was very much frightened."

Oliver Wendell was then called. He testified that Andrew was his servant.

"What is his general character for truth?"

"It is good. I have heard his testimony and believe it to be true; he gave the same relation of this matter to me on the same evening in a quarter of an hour after the affair happened, and I then asked him whether our people were to blame; he said they were."

"Pray, Sir, is it not usual for Andrew to amplify and embellish a story?"

"He is a fellow of a lively imagination, and will sometimes amuse the servants in the kitchen, but I never knew him to tell a serious lie."

Newtown Prince, a free Negro, also saw people with sticks striking the guns. "I apprehended danger and that the guns might go off accidentally," said Prince. "I went to get to the upper end of the Town Hall. They said: 'Fire, damn you, fire!' 'Fire, you lobsters, you dare not fire!'" Did he see anything thrown? "Nothing but snowballs flung by some youngsters."

Much of the testimony was confusing, largely because untrained observers are not usually accurate witnesses. Most of the men called tried to be truthful, but a handful was obviously biased and ready to distort. Chronology suffered when events were not remembered in their order of occurrence. The main outlines of the shooting were repeated so often that no one could doubt that the men who gathered in King Street were prepared to show their animosity toward the military. Townsmen admitted freely that they had come armed with sticks and swords.

Sometimes questions would make a witness cautious. There was James Brewer, who volunteered: "When I saw Dr. Young he had a sword in his hand," then immediately suffered a loss of memory.

"Was the sword naked or not?"

"I cannot remember."

"What kind of a sword was it?"

"I do not remember."

But Benjamin Burdick was quite frank about his armament. One of the soldiers "pushed at me with his bayonet," said Burdick, "which I put by with what was in my hand."

"What was it?"

"A Highland broadsword."

James Cromwell testified that he saw Killroy with a bloody bayonet; there was "blood dried on" for five or six inches. James Carter was positive it was blood. Samuel Hemmingway said he heard Killroy say he would not miss an opportunity of firing on the inhabitants. Some reports said Killroy stuck his bayonet into Gray's dead body.

In trying to show the jurors that mob action has nothing in common with earnest political activity Josiah Quincy turned to the writings of John Dickinson, whose *Letters of a Farmer of Pennsylvania to the Inhabitants of the British Colonies* had been widely read and approved, and had greatly supported the position of the moderates. He said Dickinson was "an author whom, I could wish, were in the hands of all of you." And he quoted from the Farmer: "The cause of Liberty is a cause of too much dignity to be sullied by turbulence and tumult. It ought to be maintained in a manner suitable to her nature. Those who engage in it should breathe a sedate, yet fervent spirit, animating them to actions of prudence, justice, modesty, bravery, humanity, and magnanimity." Then Quincy asked: "Was it justice or humanity to attack, insult, ridicule, or abuse a single sentry at his post? Was it either modest, brave, or magnanimous to rush upon the points of fixed bayonets, and trifle and provoke at the very mouths of muskets? It may be brutal rage, or wanted rashness, but not surely any true magnanimity."

When John Adams closed his case he described the difference between murder and manslaughter, with special reference to Montgomery. He said a soldier had the prejudices of the world against him and must defend himself against dangerous rioters. "If he was knocked down on his station, had he not reason to think his life in danger, or did it not raise his passions and put him off his guard, so that it cannot be more than manslaughter? . . . It is always safe to err on the side of mercy." This was the keynote of the defense.

When the time came for the judges to address the jury, Justice Trowbridge delivered an eloquent analysis of the different forms of homicide recognized by common law and statute law, and pointed out that "malice is the grand criterion that distinguishes murder from all other homicides." Justice Oliver was impressed by the magnanimity of Patrick Carr, who told Dr. Jeffries while dying that he bore the soldiers no malice. "This Carr was not upon oath, it is true," said the Justice, "but you will determine whether a man just stepping into eternity is not to be believed, especially in favor of a set of men by whom he had lost his life." His instructions seemed to point the way to acquittal:

"If upon the whole, by comparing the evidence, ye should find that the prisoners were a lawful assembly at the Custom House, which there can be no doubt of if you believe the witnesses; and also that they behaved properly in their own department whilst there, and did not fire till there was a necessity to do it in their own defense, —which I think there is a violent presumption of; and if on the other hand ye should find that the people who were collected around the soldiers were an unlawful assembly, and had a design to endanger, if not take away, their lives, as seems to be evident from blows succeeding threatenings, ye must in such case acquit the prisoners, and if upon the whole, ye are in any reasonable doubt of their guilt, ye

must then, agreeably to the rule of law, declare them innocent."

When the verdict was read, six soldiers—Carroll, Hartegan, McCauley, Warren, Weems, and White—were declared not guilty. Hugh Montgomery, the sentry, and
Matthew Killroy, were declared guilty of manslaughter;
Montgomery had shot Crispus Attucks, and Killroy had
shot Samuel Gray. They had the privilege of pleading
benefit of clergy, which gave them the choice of brand-
ing instead of imprisonment. They were burned on the left
thumb and discharged.

A number of years afterward Thomas Hutchinson,
writing up notes for his *History*, made a disclosure of
much pertinence that remained hidden among his papers
until Mrs. Catherine Barton Mayo published it in her *Additions to the History of the Province of Massachusetts Bay*
in the *Proceedings of the American Antiquarian Society,
1949*. Hutchinson had written that an attempt was
made to remit the burning of Montgomery because "he
had been knocked down with a club and provoked to fire
as appeared in the course of the evidence. This Montgomery afterwards acknowledged to one of his counsel that he
was the man who gave the word *fire*, which was supposed
by some of the witnesses to come from the Captain; that
being knocked down and rising again, with the agony from
the blow, he said, 'Damn you, fire,' and immediately he
fired himself and the rest followed him."

The shift from murder to manslaughter, and the acquittal of all but two of the soldiers, and those freed after
light punishment, caused great annoyance to Samuel
Adams, who had made himself the chief spokesman for the

charge that the men were guilty of murder. He held his peace until all the verdicts were in; then began writing to the news sheets, signing classical names. He criticized the verdicts, the way the cases were conducted, and the misuse of evidence. His aim remained the same—to get the military out of Boston, and to keep the patriots, especially the Sons of Liberty, in line for further demonstrations against British attacks on colonial freedom.

He called for the identity of the man in the red cloak, who had spoken to a crowd in Dock Square, after which the mob started for the main guard. He "wanted this person ascertained." But no one obliged him. He wrote in a letter signed Vindex: "They not only fired without the orders of the civil magistrate but they never called for one, which they might easily have done. They went down of their own accord, armed with muskets and bayonets fixed, presuming they were clothed with as much authority by the law of the land as the posse comitatus of the country with the high sheriff at their head."

Hutchinson characterized Adams' argument as "sophistry." He said it was unreasonable to suppose a soldier deprived himself of the right to defend himself when his life was in danger.

This trial was taken down in shorthand by John Hodgson, who "undertook the gigantic task" of making a report in full, according to John Adams, who wrote, about forty years later: "Unlike the indefatigable men of the same class in this age he gave way, completely exhausted, before he reached the end. The published report, confessedly imperfect, makes a volume of more than two hundred closely written pages. It is better in every part than in the arguments of the counsel for the defense." Here Adams was again expressing his feeling of inadequacy, a characteristic he never lost.

The court convened for the third trial on December 12. Hammond Green, Thomas Greenwood, Edward Manwaring, and John Munroe, Customs employees, had been indicted with the soldiers for murder but were to be tried separately as civilians. They had been accused of firing on the crowd from the Custom House window and balcony. Samuel Quincy appeared for the Attorney General, but L. K. Wroth and H. B. Zobel, editors of the *Legal Papers of John Adams* (1965), found no evidence of participation by John Adams, or mention of counsel for the defense. A few witnesses testified and the record says the jury acquitted the men "without going from their seats." The bench must have instructed a verdict for acquittal with the full concurrence of the Attorney General's office.

The indictment had been drawn in March, when public anger was at its peak. The original accuser was a French boy, Charles Bourgatte, a servant of Manwaring's, who had sworn that three shots had been fired from the window of the Custom House, two by himself at Manwaring's order, and one by Manwaring; there also was a shot from the balcony. The town committee, busily collecting evidence, promptly found corroboration by Samuel Drowne, but guarded itself by adding a statement by Timothy White that some thought Drowne "foolish." The accusations aroused the ire of Acting Governor Hutchinson, who said later that "the infamous French boy" had been a great distance from the scene that evening, and that the other witness was "little better than an idiot." Remarking that seven in all had sworn there was shooting from the Custom House, and that James Bowdoin, in letters, substantiated the firing, he concluded that "there is no judging, in such times, where the credulity of the people would stop."

Edward Payne swore he saw no firing from the Custom House, and three others agreed with him. Gillow Bess said he thought three or four flashes from guns seemed higher than the rest, but saw no one firing from the Custom House. He swore the indicted men had not been there that evening, nor did anyone shoot out of the window. Manwaring and Munroe had quickly established alibis and had been released; a short time later they were rearrested. The four men, all falsely accused, spent a fortnight in prison; even then the indictment was allowed to stand and they were arraigned in court, though their innocence had been established to the satisfaction of the magistrates.

The French boy retracted his story. He was arrested for perjury and sentenced to the pillory and to receive twentyfive stripes from the sheriff. When the sheriff prepared to execute the sentence a crowd collected and refused to let him proceed. Two days later he carried out the sentence.

In the third volume of Thomas Hutchinson's *History of the Province of Massachusetts Bay*, which was completed by the Governor's son, occurs this information:

"A few days after the trials, while the court continued to sit, an incendiary paper was posted up in the night upon the door of the Town House, complaining of the court for cheating the injured people with a show of justice, and

calling upon them to rise and free the world of such do-
mestick tyrants. It was taken down in the morning and carried to the court, who were much disturbed, and appealed to the Lieutenant Governor, who laid it before the
Council, and a proclamation was issued, which there was
no room to suppose would have any effect."

It is possible to get an approximation of the heated par-
tisanship of the time from the comment that the original
publisher of the *Trials* added to the book. He wrote: "The
soldiers were the first to assault, to threaten, and to apply contemptuous epithets to the inhabitants. It might
have been prudent and wise in the people to have borne
these taunts and the insolence with more patience, waiting
for relief until an act of the British Government had ordered the troops from the town. They had the spirit and
courage, however, defenseless as they were, to return
the insolent language of the soldiers, and when threatened
and attacked, to stand in their own defense. And in the
several rencontres which took place were able to repel
their assailants."

During the American Revolution, and long afterward,
no man who hoped to remain in this country would have
dared to contradict him.

IV The Years Before the Massacre

✻✻✻

1

Origins of Dissent

A VIOLENT OUTBURST of popular feeling is usually based upon what is often called "smoldering resentment." The clashes between soldiers and townsmen in Boston had been multiplying ever since the military occupation began. The baiting of the sentry, Private Hugh Montgomery of the 24th Regiment of Foot, in front of the Custom House would not have taken place if a long series of incidents had not exasperated the civilians. Issues of rights and privileges, based on constitutional grounds, and raised in the courts and the Assembly, meant less to the average townsmen than the daily spectacle of redcoated soldiers moving with a proprietary air through the streets, asking for cards of identity, and demanding "Who goes there?" of townsmen whose movements had never been challenged.

When one considers what started this feeling of irritation, one goes back a long way in colonial experiences to the very beginnings of settlement in New England. Dissent started with the charters and patents granted in the early seventeenth century, when Englishmen who had suffered discrimination for their beliefs and practices were permitted to emigrate, to the immense satisfaction of those who stayed behind. John Adams, who did a great deal of thinking about the road to independence, said the first charter, granted in the reign of James I, was more like a treaty between independent sovereigns than a charter or grant of privileges from a sovereign to his subjects. Thereafter the whittling down of the privileges of the colonists went on in many forms—with taxes on exports and imports, with laws prohibiting direct shipment to other European countries; with curtailing of manufactures that threatened to compete with British products, finally with direct tax for revenue to meet Britain's debts. There was pressure on Parliament to stop the making of caps, clothing, and even ironwork and shipbuilding in the colonies, but some of these efforts failed, and others were made inoperative by the colonial capacity for smuggling and evasion.

There is no intention to burden this chronicle with a recital of all the hardships laid upon the colonies, or all the laws enacted to draw profit from them. Touching only the high spots is sufficient to show that the effort of the British Government to tighten the controls over the activities and earnings of the colonies was continuous and forceful; that the American settlements were looked upon as plantations that worked for Britain's welfare, and that the privileges granted when the American continent was still a liability were to be withdrawn and annulled. It will be useful to mention the major acts that irritated the people of

Massachusetts, brought about the controversies between the representatives and the royal officials, and resulted in the explosions against the Writs of Assistance, the Stamp Act, and the Townshend Acts, and the long campaign against tea.

How the royalist party—the administration of the royal governor—viewed the gradual deterioration of relations between the colonists and the crown may be apprehended from a summary that Thomas Hutchinson wrote after he had departed for England, which was not published until 1949, in Catherine Barton Mayo's additions to Hutchinson's *History*. He had written: "At first the authority of Parliament seemed to be admitted, except in the course of taxes; but it was denied, in that case, upon the principle that the colonists being entitled to the rights of English subjects, no act for imposing taxes can be obligated upon them until they are represented in Parliament by persons elected by them. Upon the same principle the exception may be made to all other acts, and it soon was made to all such acts as extended the powers of the Admiralty Courts, as changed the place of trial in criminal cases, and such as made any alteration in the constitution of government, or in the interior police [policy?] of any colony, and at last the authority was denied in all cases whatever."

In 1686 the American colonies experienced the rudest shock in their history up to that time. James II had succeeded his brother, Charles II, in 1685; he was the second son of Charles I and nurtured a bitter animosity against the Puritans and liberals in religion. With this attitude and a powerful group of reactionaries supporting him, his government announced that all patents and charters held by the colonies were to be surrendered; the northern colonies were to be divided into twelve provinces and Sir Edmund Andros was to supplant the executive as governor general of the Dominion of New England. Quo warranto proceedings were begun, by the terms of which any corporation with a charter or claims to territory considered as belonging to the King, must defend that title before the Privy Council. If any claims were allowed they had to be repurchased.

Sir Edmund Andros reached Boston in December, 1686, and immediately began to rule with a high hand. He encountered the stubborn opposition of New Englanders, who already had a record of holding fast to their liberties against royal exactions. A dramatic episode of Andros' brief regime was the frustration of his attempt to seize the charter of Connecticut. He invaded a meeting of the Assembly in Hartford at the head of soldiers and demanded the charter. It was produced, but before Andros could seize it the candles were blown out and the charter disappeared in the darkness. It was hidden in the trunk of a great oak tree, which thereafter became famous as the Charter Oak. Fortunately for the colonies James had treated the British people with exactions on a par with those suffered in America, and at the end of three years he was forced off the throne. Andros was arrested and kept in the Castle off Boston, and in February, 1689, was sent back to England.

Faced by a big debt, the British government explored every possibility of getting revenue out of the colonies. The Molasses Act of 1733, which placed a duty of 6 pence on a gallon of molasses produced in the French West Indies, had been made inoperative by smuggling. New England imported molasses to make rum, and Yankee ship masters carried the rum to Africa to buy blacks from tribal chiefs and sell them in the West Indies. The new sugar act of 1763 reduced the tax to 3 pence a gallon to favor the British West Indian sugar refineries, but increased the duties on wine from Madeira and the Azores. To check smuggling Britain required all shipmasters to furnish bond, sent warships to patrol the American coast, and expropriated ships caught in illicit trade, thereby raising one-seventh of the cost of the military in the colonies. The tightening of trade regulations caused much resentment and John Adams quoted a statement that they "caused a greater alarm in the country than the taking of Fort William Henry [by the French] in the year 1757." Otis said the tax on molasses and sugar was more than sufficient to support all the Crown officials. John Adams wrote years later: "I know not why we should blush to confess that molasses was an essential ingredient in American independence."

2

Franklin Speaks for Colonial Union

THE FIRST SERIOUS plan for bringing the colonies into a
political union, in which they would act together on their
mutual interests, was proposed by Benjamin Franklin in
Albany in 1754. The occasion was a conference called for
quite another purpose—the renewal of treaties with the
Six Nations, in order to placate the Indian tribes and ce-
ment their ties with the British on the eve of hostilities with
the French. The Board of Trade had invited certain colonies to send representatives, but only seven responded:
New York, Massachusetts, Rhode Island, Connecticut,
New Hampshire, Pennsylvania, and Maryland. In real-
ity Connecticut and Rhode Island had not been invited,
but came because the subject affected their interests;
whereas New Jersey and Virginia had been invited, but
did not come. The Six Nations were the Mohawks, Onon-
dagas, Oneidas, Senecas, Cayugas, and Tuscaroras.

Before the middle of the eighteenth centry the American colonies had no political organization in common and

no serious drive for united action. The rights and privileges granted by the royal government in their charters were so different that each colony held fast to its own, and the smaller ones were apprehensive of the preponderance of the larger colonies. They had been piling up similar experiences in regulating their own affairs, repelling Indian depredations, and enduring various forms of English trade restrictions. After the Board of Trade succeeded the Lords of Trade in 1696, William Penn presented it with a plan for colonial union described as idealistic. Several of the colonies joined the war to defeat the Indian King Philip, but received no help from the others. Massachusetts provided a large contingent for Colonel William Pepperell's campaign against Louisbourg in 1745. Georgia and the Carolinas tangled with the Indians in the South. None of these campaigns engaged the colonies as a whole, nor did they foreshadow united action.

The project of a military union for mutual protection had occurred to a number of governors, notably General William Shirley of Massachusetts. New York's Governor Clinton by necessity had led in conferring with the Six Nations, and Shirley had attended conferences in Albany in 1748 and 1751. The latter was attended only by representatives of Massachusetts, Connecticut, and South Carolina, although all the colonies with a western frontier were continually losing settlers to the Indians. Shirley's views favored a union with specific quotas of men and money to be furnished by the colonies. All governors would continue to be royal appointees, and there would be no colonial representatives in Parliament.

A cartoon later widely circulated in the colonies appeared in the May 13, 1754, issue of the *New York Gazette*.

It showed a dismembered snake, with the words "Join or Die," as a warning to the colonists.

The conference convened in Albany on June 19, 1754. Coincident with the sessions with the Indians, who were led by the Mohawk chief Hendrick, Franklin offered his plan. The conference appointed a committee of seven, of which both Franklin and Thomas Hutchinson were members. They discussed the project "hand in hand with the Indian business daily," said Franklin, and out of it came a tentative proposal, which the conference ordered sent to the legislatures of all the colonies for consideration. It proposed a president general, appointed and paid by the Crown, and a grand council of fortyeight chosen by the assemblies. The council would regulate the size and use of the land forces and coast defense, levy taxes and customs duties, make appropriations, and act on civil legislation. The president general would have a veto power, appoint all military officers, and manage Indian affairs, including the development of new settlements. Thus the president general remained independent of popular control, even his salary coming from the Crown, a concession that Hutchinson was to get from the British Government against the wishes of the Massachusetts Assembly when he was governor.

Not one of the assemblies approved the plan, chiefly because none was ready to accept a superior organization that would take over some of its powers. As Franklin put it, in a much-quoted sentence, "The assemblies did not adopt it as they all thought there was too much prerogative in it, and in England it was judged to have too much of the democratic. . . . I am still of the opinion that it would have been happy for both sides of the water if it had been adopted. The colonies, so united, would have been sufficiently strong to have defended themselves; there would have been no need of troops from England; of course the subsequent pretence for taxing America and the bloody contest it occasioned would have been avoided."

At this time, twentyone years before the American Revolution, Franklin was not advocating the severance of the colonies from the mother country. Rather, he visualized them as part of the British homeland, separated merely by the Atlantic Ocean. The Appalachians were a British frontier; to bring troops from England to defend it was a costly and inefficient method. Individual colonies could not cope alone with the dangers of the frontier, but the advantages of a united front were obvious. Franklin received no encouragement. In his own state, Pennsylvania, he was practically ignored by the Assembly, and the other colonies were all too preoccupied with their provincial affairs.

3

The French and Indian War

THE SIGNIFICANCE of the French and Indian War in American history is rarely given much attention in popular accounts because the American Revolution overshadows it so mightily. It was, however, of tremendous importance to the continent, for without it the march of the Thirteen Colonies to independence would have been much harder. The "ifs" of history are of course post mortem, suitable only for speculation. The French and Indian War, known to British historians as the Seven Years' War, was one of the intermittent wars that France and England, and after 1707 Great Britain, had fought for centuries. It saddled Britain with a huge debt. It knocked the French out of North America, but the Bourbon monarchy, weakened by corruption, still could strike back, and a little more than twenty-five years later it sealed the doom of the British power in the Thirteen Colonies and enabled them to capture the vast wilderness that was once part of New France.

At this distance from the events it seems incredible that

a succession of British governments should have so mis-
managed their fiscal policies as to alienate the American
colonies. To use Pitt's famous phrase, the Americans were
the sons, not the bastards, of England. But the position of
the British is easily defined. The nation needed money to
pay its expensive operations in peace and war; the colonies
were its property and ought to carry part of the burden;
the only problem was how to get more revenue out of
them. The government did not admit that the colonies
were entitled to a voice in the imposition of taxes, or that
they were so free that they could reject any laws affecting
their administration passed by the British Parliament. Even
the men with a friendly attitude toward the colonies recognized that money must be raised, and for twenty years
after the French and Indian War Parliament, under various
ministries, tried to find ways of raising it. The repeal of the
Stamp Act and of most of the Townshend Acts disclosed
both their uncertainty over how to proceed, and a yield-
ing at times to a more lenient policy.

John Adams was one of the Massachusetts patriots who
realized that the end of the French and Indian war marked
the beginning of a concentrated attempt of the British
Government to get more revenue out of the colonies. He
has written:

"It was not until the annihilation of the French dominion in America that any British ministry had dared to gratify their own wishes, and the desire of the nation, by
projecting a formal plea for raising a national revenue
from America by parliamentary taxation. The first great
manifestation of this design was by the order to carry into
strict execution those acts of parliament which were wellknown by the appellation of the Acts of Trade, which had

been a dead letter, unexecuted for half a century, and some of them, I believe, for nearly a whole one. This produced, in 1760-1761, an awakening and a revival of American principles and feelings, which went on increasing till in 1775 it burst out in open violence, hostility, and fury."

Adams was not a firebrand, and did not advocate separation from Britain in the decades of controversy over taxation. He was, however, greatly disturbed by British blundering in peace and war. Looking back on his career in later life, he recalled that in 1755 he had deep misgivings about the way the British governed. As he put it, he had "distinct thoughts of an independency of Great Britain" and cited the miserable conduct of Shirley, Braddock, Loudoun, and other leaders in conducting the war and managing American affairs. "I ardently wished we had nothing to do with Great Britain and firmly believed that the colonies, if left to themselves, and suffered to unite, might defend themselves against the French much better without Great Britain than with her."

The French and Indian War left Great Britain burdened with a debt estimated at £140,000,000, an enormous sum at any time. To help get rid of this burden, for high interest was charged then as now, the Government studied new ways of raising revenue. It had tried for decades to increase the returns from duties on trade and shipping, and had made some efforts to stop smuggling, which was carried on universally and was hard to control. The British Government now did what all governments do when they need money: it raised rates already in effect; it devised new ways of taxing; it enlarged the machinery of collection. These methods collided with the determination of the Americans to maintain taxation for internal use as their own inherent right.

The colonies already had contributed heavily to the costs of the war. It is generally set down that New England lost 25,000 men in land actions, and other men at sea. One estimate computed the cost to the colonies at $20,000,000, when the buying power of the dollar was many times that of today. Britain at intervals had appropriated $5,409,000 to reimburse the colonies for provisions, clothing, and stores for the troops; after the war it voted another $1,000,000, but owing to disputes over revenue this sum was never paid. There also were loans to the mother country that fared much as loans did centuries later. The Provinces had other expenses not covered by the Quartering Act for which they could not collect.

The colonial assemblies could look across their western borders and observe a huge wilderness completely outside their jurisdiction and governed by a standing army under General Gage. This area, extending from the Appalachian Mountains to the Mississippi River, had come to Great Britain as the spoils of the French and Indian War. This was Indian land, coveted by audacious settlers and irresponsible exploiters, and filled with threats of bloody clashes with Indian tribes. In order to consolidate their gains the British had to keep the Indians friendly. This meant regulating immigration and settlement into this vast area, something that the separate colonies, burdened with their own fiscal problems and unified neither in border defense nor administration, could not do. Lord Shelburne, president of the Board of Trade during part of the Grenville ministry, proposed that to hold the peace with the Indians it was necessary to keep white settlers out of their territory. So Grenville in October, 1763, announced in a proclamation that no one would be allowed to move west of the Appalachians. This did not affect New England as much as the middle Atlantic colonies, but it was an example of the desperation of the ministry before its huge task. The exclusion was completely unworkable because the border could not be patrolled. Colonials continued to push into the Indian lands, and fighting with the Indians went on for another hundred years, until the tribes were cowed or dispossessed.

4

James Otis and the Writs of Assistance

ONE OF THE ROYAL devices for collecting customs duties that caused increasing resentment in the years before the American Revolution was the writ of assistance. By its means a commissioner of customs obtained authority from a court to search for "uncustomed" goods—goods that had evaded customs duties—taking with him a constable or other peace officer. As no specific object of search had to be stated, the writ authorized attempts to pry into private affairs on mere suspicion, or no suspicion at all, merely to increase the royal revenues. The use of the writs produced vehement opposition among merchants, who held to the traditional Anglican conviction that a man's house was his castle. Even the argument that such search had to be made to uncover smuggling did not mitigate the intrusion.

Writs of assistance had been used since the days of

Charles II and had caused irritation in England. When the British Treasury was forced to raise more money to pay the nation's big debt, it put pressure on the customs service of the colonies, and encouraged use of the writs. The power a writ gave a commissioner was quite extraordinary; without having to announce what he was looking for he could enter any ship bottom, boat or other vessel, and in the daytime any house, cellar, warehouse or other shelter, and in the case of resistance "break open any door, trunk, chest, case, pack, truss, or other parcel or package whatsoever for any goods, wares, or merchandise," and if he found articles on which duty had not been paid he was to seize them and transfer to the customs warehouse for the King's disposition.

In 1755 Thomas Paxton, Surveyor General of Customs, was authorized to use writs by the Superior Court and did so at intervals until 1760, when King George II died. According to the law, such writs had to be renewed under a new king. By this time the writs of assistance were part of the mounting grievances of colonial merchants who were on the alert for new attempts to enforce them. When James Cockle, a Salem commissioner, applied to the Superior Court in session at Essex for authority to use the writ a storm of criticism broke and Chief Justice Stephen Sewall, who had doubts about the constitutionality of the law, ordered the hearing on the application to be carried over to the next session of the court in Boston. Faced with the prospect of renewed use of the writs, about sixty merchants combined to oppose the petition of the customs official in court.

The Commissioner of Customs asked James Otis, Jr., Advocate General in the Court of Vice Admiralty, to argue the case for the writs, but he misjudged his man. Otis flared up with indignation. He hated blanket writs as an invasion of private rights. With patriotic fervor he resigned as Advocate and determined to lead the fight against them, with Oxenbridge Thacher as associate. "In such a cause I despise all fear," announced Otis.

This legal action now acquired unexpected importance in the campaign for colonial liberty, and since then has become a historic milestone in the fight for independence because of an inference John Adams drew from it. The Boston bar was interested in the confrontation of Otis and Chief Justice Hutchinson, for a personal reason. The post of Chief Justice, which was filled by appointment by the Governor, became vacant when Sewall died suddenly before the petition could be heard. The hope of the liberal faction of the bar was that Colonel James Otis, father of James, would be appointed to the bench, and it was understood that former Governor Shirley had promised to support him. But Governor Bernard named Thomas Hutchinson, thereby retaining tight control of the Court. It was assumed that the younger Otis, already known for his vehemence in public speech, would hardly be restrained when he confronted the man who had displaced his father. But Otis did not air his resentment.

When the case was called in the Council chamber the place was packed with merchants who opposed the application and members of the bar. John Adams who had not yet been admitted to the bar, had come in order to transcribe the arguments. Jeremiah Gridley, Attorney General, who had been the mentor of both Otis and Adams, spoke for the writ, asserting that there were times when officials needed special help in the collection of duties and citing a long list of precedents from former reigns. Oxenbridge Thacher, in opposition, stressed that the writs were acts of the British Court of Exchequer, and since that court had no authority in Boston the Superior Court could not assume its functions. This argument was also pounded home by James Otis, who called on the Court for its warrant from the Court of Exchequer, which could not be produced.

Otis then launched into the major part of his address, which, especially in the opinion of John Adams, was one of the great presentations of the time. In what Adams described as "that close, concise, nervous and energetic language" Otis summarized the constitutional grounds on which the patriots of Massachusetts based their whole legal position against taxation and regulation by Parliament. He went back to the charters to show that the Americans had been given rights to conduct their internal affairs. John Adams wrote about his address: "His observations carried irresistible conviction to the minds and hearts of many others as well as to mine, that every one of these statutes, from the navigation act to the last act of trade, was a violation of all the charters and compacts between the two countries, was a fundamental invasion of our essential rights, and was consequently null and void; that the legislatures of the colonies, and especially of Masuachusetts, had the sole and exclusive authority of legislation and especially of taxation in America."

As for the writ of assistance, Otis said that being general in its authority to search, it was illegal. "It is a power that places the liberty of every man in the hands of every petty officer. I say that I admit that special writs of assistance, to search special places, may be granted to certain persons on oath; but I deny that the writ now prayed for can be granted . . . In the first place, the writ is universal, being directed to 'all and singular justices, sheriffs and constables, and all other officers and subjects,' so that in short it is directed to every subject in the King's dominions. Everyone with this writ may be a tyrant, if this commission is legal, a tyrant in a legal manner also may control, inform, or murder anyone within the realm. In the next place, it is perpetual; there is no return. A man is accountable to no power for his doings. Third, a man with this writ in the daytime may enter all houses, shops, etc., at will and command all to assist him. Fourth, not only deputies but even their menial servants are allowed to lord it over us. Bare suspicion without oath is sufficient. An act against the constitution is void."

Otis talked for three hours, and as he paced up and down before the judges, sitting on the bench in their scarlet cloaks tipped with ermine and their long wigs of authority, he impressed everyone with the seriousness of the liberal opposition to the methods of the British Government. John Adams has described the dedicated champion of individual freedom in action:

"From the navigation acts the advocate passed to the acts of trade, and these, he contended, imposed taxes—enormous, burthensome, intolerant taxes; on this topic he gave full scope to his talent for powerful declamation and invective, against *the tyranny of taxation without representation*. From the energy with which he argued this position, that taxation without representation is tyranny, it came to be a common maxim in the mouth of everyone. And with him it formed the basis of all his speeches and political writings; he builds all his opposition to arbitrary measures from this foundation, and perpetually recurs to it through

his whole career, as the great constitutional theme of liberty, and as the fundamental principle of all opposition to
arbitrary power."

When Otis' vehemence finally subsided, and the justices
were able to pull themselves together, Chief Justice Hutchinson announced that as the practice in England was not
known, it was thought best to postpone the hearing to the
next term, and thus have an opportunity to find out.

Postponement is always deflating. It is not hard to imagine the feelings with which Otis, Thacher, John Adams,
and the Boston merchants who fought the petition, heard
the words of the Chief Justice. As might have been expected, word came from England that the Superior Court
in Boston had jurisdiction and powers similar to those of
the Court of Exchequer in Britain. The Court approved
the use of the writs on December 5, 1761. However, the
Customs Office did not press its advantage at this time, and
John Adams surmised that the royal administration did not
dare enforce the writs.

The spectacle of James Otis, Jr., leading a three-hour
battle before the Court in Boston, has been dramatized
many times in patriotic writings, but in recent years inquis-
itive historians have searched for better evidence than John
Adams' exuberance. Why, they ask, was there no notice in
the newspapers, no comment on the case in the other colonies? The "crowded courtroom", somewhat refurbished,
exists today in the Old State House; it could hardly have
held one hundred persons. Nothing appeared in print until
the *Worcester Spy* published a description that appeared to
be based on Adams' notes—in 1773, twelve years after the
hearing. Adams must have talked about the case to his
associates, but he did not write his famous report until

William Tudor, in 1818, asked for his recollections—fifty-seven years after! Given this incentive Adams pulled out all the stops.

Otis, said Adams, "was a flame of fire, with a promptitude of classical allusions, a depth of research, a rapid summary of historical events and dates, a profusion of legal authorities, a prophetic glance of the eyes into futurity, and a rapid torrent of impetuous eloquence; he harried away all before him. American independence was then and there born. The seeds of patriots and heroes . . . to defend the vigorous youth, were then and there sown. Then and there was the first scene of the first act of opposition to the arbitrary claims of Great Britain. Then and there the child Independence was born."

It was, as one historian commented, "a rare and felicitous force of memory." It came from a man of 83, who lived to be 90.

But the effort to use the writs of assistance did not end in 1761. The controversy flared up anew in the other colonies after the Townshend Revenue Act of 1767 authorized the use of the writs in order to locate dutiable goods. The secretary of the Board of Customs Commissioners in Boston instructed the principal customs officials in the ports of America to get authority to use the writs from the courts through the office of the attorney general. The petitions for a blanket authority met with obstruction and delay in a number of colonies. It was evident that the judges had studied the issue thoroughly and were unwilling to grant search warrants unless specific objectives were named under oath. There was repeated assertion that the form of the writ, which reproduced the one in use in England, was not proper for the colonies. In New York, where Robert R.

Livingston was a presiding justice of the Supreme Court, five years of delay ended with Livingston refusing to issue new writs. In Philadelphia the Chief Justice, a Tory, refused to issue any writ for a general, unspecified search, even after he had been instructed by the attorney general of England.

The biggest battle against the writs took place in Virginia, and the principles defended there eventually influenced the basic documents of the United States. Professor O. M. Dickerson, whose research uncovered pertinent data for his study, "Writs of Assistance as a Cause of the Revolution," contributed to *The Era of the American Revolution*, (1939), writes: "What happened in Massachusetts is tame compared with the struggle in Virginia. Here was an unyielding, unanimous court, convinced as to the soundness of its legal position and refusing to be moved from that position by argument, threats, or the most impressive array of legal talent from England . . . Virginia became the leader of the movement to prohibit forever the use of general warrants and unreasonable searches."

When the Bill of Rights was voted as an amendment to the Constitution of the United States, Article IV outlawed search and seizure except on oath, with specific description of the place to be searched and persons or objects to be seized. In this way the founders of the nation tried to safeguard the rights of the individual, in a battle that is constantly renewed, even down to this day.

5

The Stamp Act Riots

THE STAMP TAX had been proposed a number of times in
the House of Commons, and even Benjamin Franklin had
approved it in theory at the Albany conference of 1754.
William Pitt had opposed it because he believed no English
subjects should be taxed without their consent, and drew
the line between external and internal taxation much as the
Americans did. But in 1764 Pitt was ill and out of office, and
George Grenville, former Chancellor of the Exchequer,
became the King's First Minister. His aim was to hold the
favor of the King, who long had been urging tighter controls on colonial income. By February, 1765, Grenville had
enough backing to pass a comprehensive stamp act.

The Stamp Act affected so many public papers and documents that it touched practically all media used in fiscal,
legal, and mercantile transactions. There was practically
no scrap of paper in public use that was not expected to
bear the royal approval in the form of a stamp. The speci-
fications enumerated at the start of forty paragraphs were
so offensive that the colonials considered the document a
deviously constructed insult. The preamble said a tax must

be paid on every skin, or piece of vellum, or parchment, or sheet or piece of paper on which certain matters were engrossed, written or printed, and the tax varied considerably. Legal papers cost from six pence to two shillings; the certificate of a college degree, 2 pounds; a summans, 1 shilling; a commission for a private ship of war, 20 shillings; any franchise granted by governor, council or assembly, 6 pounds; a license for retailing wine, 4 pounds; employment worth more than 20 pounds a year, 4 pounds; and there were numerous taxes of a few shillings to be affixed to documents in general use.

The act specifies that the amounts raised "shall be paid into his majesty's treasury and there held in reserve, to be used from time to time by the Parliament, for the purpose of defraying the expenses necessary for the defense, protection and security of the said colonies and plantations." Thus out of the money paid by the colonies would come all the salaries and expenses of commissioners, and officials of the provincial government. The British government could apply the tax revenue to practically anything under its definition.

Street brawls, rioting, ransacking of private houses, became common in Boston during 1765. There was so great an interval between enactment of the Stamp Act on March 22, and the date it was to go into effect, November 1, 1765, that the patriots had plenty of time to arouse opposition. Samuel Adams and James Otis, Jr., were in the forefront of those who were using all their powers of persuasion to get their fellow townsmen to reject the stamps. Even the clergy found scriptural basis for political implications. Some of this argument filtered down to what John Adams called the lower class, and to the gangs that were always ready for a "rumpus"; 200 years later this is called a "rumble." But there was evidence that some otherwise balanced townsmen joined the rabble and gave vent to their suppressed feelings. Hanging of effigies of hated officials and burning of the effigies, sometimes in front of the subjects' homes, were the beginnings of attacks on individuals that in the ensuing years developed into tar and feathers for excise men.

More reasonable leaders opposed such behavior as inconsistent with patriotic aims. John Adams commented in his diary: "I have learned enough to show me, in all their dismal colors, the deceptions to which the people in their passion are liable, and the total suppression of equity and humanity in the human breast when thoroughly heated and hardened by party spirit."

In February, 1765, Colonel Isaac Barré, a member of Parliament who had consistently defended the American stand, resented in the House of Commons a patronizing speech by Charles Townshend. In rebutting the latter's implication that Americans were ungrateful children nurtured and protected by England, Colonel Barré called them sons of liberty. The patriots who met in Boston taverns immediately called themselves Sons of Liberty, but the term Liberty Boys long had been used. During the summer the Sons met under a large elm tree in the heart of town, which became known as the Liberty Tree. On the morning of August 14 two effigies were seen hanging from the tree—one of Andrew Oliver, Secretary of the Province, who was to have charge of the distribution of the stamps, and the other of a boot with a devil with horns sticking out at the top, a play on Lord Bute, the King's friend and adviser. In the evening the effigies were taken down and the crowd marched with them past the Town House, where the officials, including Oliver, were in session, yelling their opposition to the stamps. The rioters then went to Oliver's private dock and tore apart a half-complete structure that was to store the stamps. After burning the effigies they proceeded to Oliver's house, tearing up his garden and entering the house. Lieutenant Governor Hutchinson arrived with the Sheriff and tried to stop the mob, but order was not restored until Oliver himself appeared on his second-story balcony and promised to resign as stamp distributor. This he did later under the Liberty Tree.

Boston streets were quiet for a week or more, and then the Sons and their adherents were again eager for direct action. They were about to enter the house of Charles Paxton, Marshal of the Court of Vice Admiralty and strong supporter of the stamps, when a friend assured the men Paxton was away and invited them to partake of a barrel of punch in a tavern. Thus warmed they went to the house of William Story, Registrar of the Court, and tossed out all his records, and then proceeded to the house of Benjamin Hallowell, Controller of Customs, and treated it in the same manner.

By midnight the mob was completely out of control. Its next object was the fine town house of Lieutenant Governor Hutchinson in North Square. This official had supported many of the obnoxious rulings of the home government but, as it happened, had not favored the Stamp Act; this, however, did not deter the rioters. Hutchinson, who had been warned of their coming, ordered his two sons and two daughters to go to the house of his sister, but his daughter Sallie refused to let him face the mob alone, so he left with her. The mob then proceeded to tear the interior apart. Chairs and tables were tossed out and smashed; only the kitchen was left undamaged. Portraits went out of the windows; personal possessions, silver plate, clothing, followed; even money was thrown about, to be found next morning with the plate in the street. Hutchinson possessed a fine library and had a collection of documents on which he was basing his *History of the Province of Massachusetts Bay*. All these articles were thrown out, including one manuscript volume of the history. Hutchinson testified later that many of the magistrates and the field officers of the militia stood by during this ransacking of the house, unwilling to interfere.

When Hutchinson arrived next morning to sit on the bench of the Superior Court as Chief Justice, he appeared in the informal attire he had worn when he fled from his house the evening before. In a voice shaken by emotion he faced the courtroom and declared: "I call God to witness that I never in New England or Old, in Great Britain or America, aided or supported what is commonly called the Stamp Act, but did all in my power to prevent it. This is not declared through timidity; I have nothing to fear. They can only take away my life . . . I hope all will see how easily the people may be deluded, inflamed, carried away with madness against an innocent man. I pray God give us better hearts."

Hutchinson was aware that the Stamp Act "had disturbed the minds of the people," but he also knew that when indignation touched off emotional frenzy many other feelings entered into mob action. "In such a state of affairs," he said, "the vicious, the abandoned, have a peculiar opportunity of gratifying their corrupt affections of envy, malice and revenge." As an author he had the strongest regrets over the misuse of his manuscripts. He has phrased a fine statement of the dedication of the writing man to his tasks, which appears in the second volume of his *History:* "The perusal of the materials from which I composed my work, especially the letters and papers of our first planters, afforded me a very sensible pleasure. We are fond of prolonging our lives to the utmost length. Going back to so familiar an acquaintance with those who have lived before us approaches the nearest to it of anything we are capable of, and is, in some sort, living with them."

Luckily some of his work was retrieved. After the destruction of his home he had no hopes of getting back any part of the history, but a neighbor, the Reverent Andrew Eliot, who picked up some of the books and papers, found all but eight or ten sheets of the manuscript, which was legible although it had been lying in the street during rain. Although Hutchinson said his most valuable materials were lost he managed to reconstruct the missing parts, and eventually the three volumes of his book were published, an invitation to meet "those who have lived before us."

The ruthless attack on Hutchinson's house was just about more than the sensible patriots could stand. Samuel Adams had worked up considerable indignation against the Stamp Act among the townsmen, but he had appealed to their reason and always had used legal methods to oppose the government. He was baffled by the excesses, and so, too, must have been the clergymen who had preached opposition to the customs duties. If Adams did know the temper of the Sons of Liberty, he evidently did not abet their wild behavior. The next day he was one of the leaders who expressed their regret and anger at a meeting in Faneuil Hall. John Adams had found "universal consternation" on the faces and wrote a friend: "I voted to assist the magistrates to their utmost in preventing or suppressing any further disorder."

The town made a half-hearted attempt to curb the rioters by arresting eight and placing them in jail. But their detention lasted only overnight; the next morning someone opened the door and they walked out. The ringleader Macintosh, tried to excuse his conduct by saying he had been inflamed by a sermon against the Stamp Act preached by the Reverend Jonathan Mayhew in West Church, using for his text: "I would that they were even cut off that trouble you." Mayhew was so conscience-stricken that he sent a note of apology to Hutchinson, who remarked wryly that Mayhew might have quoted the rest of the text: "For brethren ye have been called unto liberty; only use not liberty for an occasion of the flesh, but by love serve one another." Biblical phrases were often quoted during the eighteenth century, and in the nineteenth they became the principal tools of political oratory, but Samuel Adams, John Adams, and James Otis used them sparingly. Wiser heads among the Sons of Liberty worked to keep their noisy followers in bounds, and the serious rioting stopped.

Reimbursement of the officials for their losses, so quickly agitated by conscience-stricken townsmen the day after the damage, lagged as time went on. The House of Commons urged the Province to provide restitution and Governor Bernard presented the Massachusetts Assembly with a demand for $12,000 for Hutchinson, $1,446 for Hallowell, $646 for Oliver, and $225 for Story. The Assembly voted the amounts reluctantly and added a provision that all implicated in the rioting receive amnesty.

The uproar that resulted in the colonies was not limited to Boston, which is the locale of this chronicle, but extended to New York, New Jersey, Pennsylvania, Virginia, South Carolina and other colonies. However divided by internal issues, boundary disputes, and trade jealousies, the colonies were united in condemning the Stamp Tax as an unjustifiable imposition on top of the costs incurred by the French and Indian War, and the subscriptions raised by several of the colonies, for which they had not been reimbursed.

It was the Stamp Act that prompted Patrick Henry's famous declaration beginning "Caesar had his Brutus," in a speech supporting the Virginia Resolves, which announced, as emphatically as any dictum by Samuel Adams, that Virginia and not Parliament had the right to enact taxes. Years later, when Henry's speech was a classic oration of American schoolboys, John Adams asked querously why it should have become famous, when a defiance practically identical had been spoken in the Massachusetts House at about the same time. James Otis' remonstrance to the Governor in 1762, three years before Henry's oration, had evoked similar cries of "Treason! Treason!" when read in the House.

Adoption of the Stamp Act led the New York Whigs to urge a united protest by the colonies. Acting quickly, James Otis, Jr., had the Massachusetts House invite the other colonies to send representatives to New York on October 7, 1765. Nine colonies sent men and four others agreed to abide by their action, but not all endorsed what was done. Robert R. Livingston drafted *A Petition to the*

King; Otis wrote a *Memorial to the Houses of Parliament*; also adopted was a *Declaration of Rights*. Timothy Ruggles, of Massachusetts, who presided, refused to go along and was openly reprimanded by the Speaker of the Massachusetts House. He sided later with the Tories and organized a Loyalist regiment.

Parliament was astonished by the hostility aroused by the act, but the protests of the Americans made less of an impact than the complaints of British merchants and importers, who had their business curtailed by the nonimportation campaign of the colonies. The Marquis of Rockingham, who had succeeded Grenville as First Minister, determined to lead a movement for repeal. This had the powerful support of William Pitt, the great Whig leader who in 1766 became the Earl of Chatham and took a seat in the House of Lords. The popular leaders in the colonies always had been grateful to Pitt for his recognition of the right to tax themselves. He said: "Taxation is no part of the governing or legislative power. The taxes are a voluntary gift and grant of the colonies alone. The colonies of America, represented in their several assemblies, have ever been in possession of this, their constitutional right, of giving and granting their own money. At the same time this kingdom, as the supreme governing and legislative power, has always bound the colonies by her laws, by her restrictions in trade, in navigation, in manufactures, in everything except taking their money out of their pockets without their consent."

It was during these years that the liberals and radicals began to call themselves Whigs, and the term Tories was used for those supporting the royal measures. Hutchinson wrote in his *History* that those who supported the government "were branded with the name of Tories, always the term of reproach."

The repeal of the Stamp Act had the approval of the King and was voted and signed March 18, 1766. The news did not reach Boston until May 13 because all communication was by sail. There was great jubilation, and statues to Pitt were voted in New York City, Charleston, South Carolina, and several other towns. The merchants of London apparently were equally pleased. Accompanying the repeal, however, was a Declaratory Act, which embodied the views of Pitt concerning British ownership and control of the American colonies. It hardly coincided with the opinions of home rule held by such colonial leaders as Samuel Adams and James Otis. Benjamin Franklin had a clear concept of British power and expressed the opinion that Britons had been exploiting the colonies for decades in numerous petty ways, and that they did not intend to give up their numerous indirect taxes and restrictions on trade that benefited England.

6

From Townshend to Tea

From the repeal of the Stamp Act in 1766 to the Boston Massacre in 1770, the relations between the Province of Massachusetts and Great Britain became steadily worse. Whatever hopes had been raised by Pitt's intercession were dashed when his continuing illness from gout made his attendance as First Minister impossible. Despite the efforts of members of Parliament friendly to America, the House of Commons had about a two-thirds majority for repressive measures. It determined to put into effect the Declaratory Act that the colonies were subordinate to Britain, and to tighten controls.

Charles Townshend had been named Chancellor of the Exchequer by Pitt; he had worked with Grenville on the Stamp Act and other fiscal matters that were still in force. After repeal he still faced the big deficit and had to devise ways of meeting it. There is a story that at a social gathering Grenville taunted Townshend after the latter had boasted he would find ways to tax the colonies. "You are cowards,

you dare not tax America!" said Grenville, and Townshend retorted: "I dare tax America!" Grenville, still
smarting over his defeat, replied: "I wish to God I could
see it."

Townshend decided that the best way to raise revenue
was by import-export duties, rather than by internal
taxes, such as stamp acts. He knew that a large amount of
revenue was lost by smuggling and corruption, and determined to stop the leaks. In June-July, 1767, he had Parliament pass a group of acts to these ends. One act placed duties on paper, glass, painters' colors, lead, and tea. A second act reduced the export tax on a pound of tea from a
shilling to three pence, in order to increase consumption.
An act also removed duties on grain and whale oil paid
by colonials in Britain and gave bounties on hemp, flax,
and timber from the colonies.

Next came the reorganization of the customs administration. A law established the American Board of Customs
Commissioners, to have its headquarters in Boston but be
staffed entirely by agents appointed in England and paid
by the Exchequer. This removed a large number of employees who were notorious for exploiting the customs
service for their own gain. Everyone knew that smuggling
was general and Boston profited by it. The cries of anguish that arose throughout the colonies over this law
were supposed to emanate because the Americans resented
legislation by Parliament that disregarded their right to tax
themselves, but historians say many of the protests came
from merchants and others who had vested interests in
evading the duties. What made matters worse was the en-
dorsement of the use of writs of assistance to uncover
goods that had bypassed the customs. This was the hated

practice of getting a court order to search for hidden goods without specifying what the officer was looking for. This had been denounced in the memorable court hearing of 1761, when James Otis had made his impassioned speech against it. The writ was still in force, but the new reference to it stirred up all the old animosity. Moreover, most of the cases that came under the Acts of Trade and Navigation were to be tried in Vice Admiralty courts, without the use of juries. British officials opposed American juries, which they accused of bias, and this became another grievance that the patriots held against the administration. The British Government also expected to draw on its new revenue to pay the salaries of the civil list, including governors, judges and other appointees, who now drew their salaries from appropriations by the Assembly and hence were obligated to the people. This became a fighting issue that caused protest meetings right up to the eve of the Revolution, for the Americans now saw their own civil administration taken from them piecemeal.

Townshend died before his acts were fully enforced. In January, 1768, Lord Hillsborough was given expanded duties as Secretary of State for the Colonies. The Massachusetts House now acted to get support from the other colonies for united protests against the British exactions. Prodded by Samuel Adams, on February 4 it appointed a committee on which Adams, James Otis, Thomas Cushing and other liberals were members, to draft a communication to all the assemblies of the colonies and the House of Burgesses of Virginia, suggesting that they harmonize their efforts. The letter criticised the appointment of customs commissioners in Britain, the proposal to pay officials from Crown funds, and the Quartering Act, which required the people to pay the expenses of the King's "marching troops," not standing army.

The circular letter had unexpected repercussions. Lord Hillsborough received it in April and immediately characterized it as seditious and "a most dangerous and factious tendency, calculated to inflame the minds of good subjects and promote unwarrantable combination." He asked the governors of all the colonies to take no notice of it, and then gave Governor Bernard two instructions: to demand that the Assembly rescind the letter, and to dismiss it if it refused. Bernard conveyed the first part of the letter, and on Samuel Adams' insistence, disclosed the second part. Adams had the satisfaction of reading it to the Assembly, quite sure of his position because of promises of support coming in from some of the other colonies. James Otis, Jr., then delivered one of his fiery denunciations of the British ministry, which John Adams thought superior to Patrick Henry's famous "Caesar had his Brutus" speech, and led some conservatives to consider it pretty close to treason. Said Otis: "When Lord Hillsborough knows that we will not rescind our acts he should apply to Parliament to rescind theirs. Let Britons rescind their measures, or they are lost forever."

The members of the House were full of fight. They adopted resolutions denouncing interference by royal officials and then voted 92 to 17 against rescinding the circular letter. This caused the Sons of Liberty great elation. They celebrated the "immortal 92" and ridiculed the seventeen on every occasion. Paul Revere made a silver punch bowl with "92" and other symbols on it. Boston associated its defiance with the case of militant John Wilkes, English journalist and politician, who was conducting one of his periodic campaigns against the House of Commons, of which he was at different times an unwelcome member. The admiration of many American dissidents for Wilkes is responsible for the name of Wilkes-Barre, in which the name of Colonel Isaac Barré, who helped defeat the Stamp Act in Parliament, is also commemorated.

The Assembly continued in session to consider the attitude of Governor Bernard. He had abetted curtailing the liberties and privileges conferred on the Province by its charter. The members made a list of his acts and petitioned the King to remove him from office. Governor Bernard dissolved the Assembly, then and later giving evidence of his exasperation.

Samuel Adams was determined at this time to keep all opposition to the inequitable legislation of Parliament on a legal basis. He considered a pledge by merchants not to import certain articles as a legitimate device to make the demands of the colony felt in London. He was quick to spread ominous warnings of dire things to come, but he deprecated talk of revolt. While trying to influence the ministries abroad he also had to keep his home front in line. Not all merchants who resented the taxes were ready to support nonimportation, for without goods from abroad they had little to sell. The Sons of Liberty brought pressure to bear on them and they suffered both indignities and loss of trade.

Nonimportation continued for the next few years and was still being pursued by the time of the Boston Massacre in 1770. The incident of John Hancock's sloop *Liberty*, an open defiance of the Commissioner of Customs, precipitated the entry of the two British Regiments in Boston on September 27, 1768.

The nonimportation campaign against British goods was variously effective, cutting down trade in Massachusetts, New York, and the North generally, and less so in the South. It caused enough distress among English merchants to make them want the obnoxious taxes abolished. In January, 1770, Lord North, Chancellor of the Exchequer after Townshend's death, became the King's First Minister. He was responsive to the pleas of the merchants and supported a bill to repeal the Townshend duties except that on tea. By a coincidence it was called up in the House of Commons on March 5, 1770, the day of the Boston Massacre. But after that tragic event nonimportation was more strongly supported in the colonies.

Typical of the resolutions adopted by Massachusetts towns is that of Roxbury, which was voted on March 5. It said that since the merchants and traders of Boston and almost all the maritime towns on the continent were sacrificing their private interests by not importing British goods until the Townshend Act was repealed, Roxbury would assist "in every constitutional way" to make the agreement effective. And Roxbury viewed, "with the utmost abhorrence and detestation the little, mean and sordid conduct of a few traders in this province, who have and still do import British goods contrary to said agreement, and have thereby discovered that they are governed by a selfish spirit, and are regardless of, and deaf to, the miseries and calamities which threaten this people."

The resolution then listed the names of individuals and firms in Boston, Hatfield, and Marlborough that ignored the agreement and added: "We do hereby declare that we will not buy the least article of any of said persons ourselves, or suffer any acting for or under us, to buy of them;

neither will we buy of those that shall buy or exchange any articles of goods with them. . . . That to the end the generations which are yet unborn may know who they were that laughed at the distresses and calamities of this people, and instead of striving to save their country when in imminent danger, did strive to render ineffectual a virtuous and commendable plan, the names of these importers shall be annually read at the March meeting . . . That we will not make use of any foreign teas in our several families until the revenue acts are repealed, case of sickness excepted."

One of the Boston importers condemned in this resolution was Theophilus Lillie, who was being harassed by the patriots to bring him into line. When John Adams passed Lillie's place of business on February 22, 1770, he saw that they had erected a wooden plank, with a head crudely painted thereon and a hand pointing to the house. On it were the names of three importers who were ignoring the nonimportation agreement. Later in the day a neighbor named Ebenezer Richardson resented the object and tried to tear it down. This brought together a group of boys and men who jeered at Richardson and threw mud and stones at his windows. Thereupon Richardson appeared at an upper window with a gun and fired pointblank into the crowd. He struck and killed a boy named Christopher Snider, son of a poor German immigrant.

Richardson was apprehended before the infuriated crowd could seize him. In his *History* Hutchinson wrote: "Having been a land-waiter or inferior custom house official, and before that an informer against illicit traders, he was peculiarly obnoxious to the people." The funeral of the Snider boy on February 26 was raised to the status of a great anti-British demonstration, led by the Sons of Liberty, and thousands of Bostonians joined. "Innocence itself is not safe" was one of the legends laid on the coffin. The cortege formed at the Liberty Tree, where John Adams joined it, and was preceded by several hundred schoolboys. A journal called Snider the first martyr in the cause of American liberty. Richardson was tried and convicted of murder on April 21 but Lieutenant Governor Hutchinson refused to sign his death warrant, and after two years in prison Richardson was pardoned by the King.

The place that tea holds in the history of American independence must astonish those sons of Europe who have provided the bulk of American population since the great immigrations of the nineteenth century. There are many millions of American citizens who have no kinship with the Anglican community of eighteenth century Massachusetts, but who benefit in their present circumstances from the principles of democratic government for which these forerunners fought the tax on tea. Americans today are not a nation of tea-drinkers; they tax tea on entry and pay a sales tax on tea when they buy it; they accept freely taxes on all sorts of necessities; they pay direct and indirect taxes, imposed by several authorities on identical possessions, and endure the acceleration of the taxes without protest. But in 1769-1775 tea was a fighting issue because the principle was of greater importance to life, liberty, and the pursuit of happiness than the commodity itself.

V   Issues After the Massacre

✳✳✳

1

Paul Revere and the Famous Print

WE ALL KNOW him for his remarkable horsemanship on the midnight of April 19, 1775. But actually Paul Revere contributed another, and possibly more influential, episode to American history when he engraved and printed a sketch called *The Bloody Massacre perpetrated in King Street Boston on March 5th 1770 by a party of the 29th Regt.*

It was the most effective demonstration of the vicious character of the British military that could have been devised. It represented a squad of grenadiers firing a volley point blank into a crowd of unarmed civilians, several of whom lay prostrate. It had more power in swaying the common citizen than a dozen harangues by Samuel Adams. As a picture it spoke eloquently to the illiterate— and there were many worthy sons of New England who could not read. It appeared twenty days after the catastrophe it purported to illustrate, and it has been reproduced innumerable times in schoolbooks, histories and encyclopedias, during the last two hundred years.

However, as a picture of what actually occurred, it is basically inaccurate. And there is good evidence that Paul Revere appropriated the design from Henry Pelham.

The setting is dominated by the facade and tower of the Town House facing King Street, with two-story buildings converging toward it from left and right. At the right what was probably the Custom House, with the roof of a sentry box showing, is labelled Butcher's Hall. In the right foreground seven British soldiers fire their muskets at a crowd of civilians, none of whom carries a club or weapon of any kind. Three men are down, one is being carried off. Behind the soldiers the commanding officer raises his sword to order the firing. A puff of smoke comes out of a window of Butcher's Hall, with the barrel of a gun showing. In the center foreground a dog stands placidly viewing the scene.

This, then, was not a representation of the shooting, nor was it intended to be that. It was a piece of propaganda engraved by Paul Revere, ardent Son of Liberty, and endorsed by practically all the patriots who were determined to get the British soldiers out of the country. Such one-sided interpretation of actual events was by no means unusual. Before the coming of photography objective rendering of spectacles was unknown and unlooked for, and formal portraiture was invariably complimentary. Physical blemishes were left to caricature, which intentionally made them worse. In the case of the "horrid massacre," the Sons of Liberty recognized only murderous soldiers and peaceful, protesting townsmen.

Immediately after the shooting in King Street Paul Revere received an order from Edes & Gill for engravings of four coffins bearing the initials of the first four victims, for publication in the *Gazette*. This completed, Edes & Gill sponsored the engraving of the Boston massacre, which connoisseurs have called the most famous of American prints. After Revere had published this print on March 25, twenty days after the tragedy, someone must have pointed out that the clock on a house in the background gave the time as 8, whereas it was well known that the shooting took place much later. Revere immediately doctored his plate, and the next impression showed the clock at 10:20, which is nearer the actual time. He also corrected a few errors in the text that accompanied the sketch. This alteration made the first draft a rarity, and indeed only one copy is extant, this being the property of J. William Middendorf II, a collector who has specialized in Americana.

What was Paul Revere doing on the fateful night of March 5, 1770? Miss Esther Forbes, author of *Paul Revere and the World He Lived In*, who has accounted for his movements practically from day to day, replies: "We do not know." In her biography she surmises that he may have been a part of the crowd, or, like many others, he may have "grabbed a bucket, rushed out to a fire, and found a massacre."

The reason biographers would like to know what connection Revere had with the tragedy is that about one hundred years after the event evidence came to light that Revere had appropriated the design for his print from a guileless associate. After Edes & Gill announced that they had for sale the engraving made by Paul Revere, Henry Pelham, himself artist and engraver, and half-brother of John Singleton Copley, wrote Revere a stinging letter accusing him of stealing Pelham's design. Dated Thursday morning, Boston, March 29, 1770, the essential paragraph reads:

> To Mr. Paul Revere, Present,—
> Sir: When I heard that you was cutting a plate of the late Murder I thought it impossible as I knew you was not capable of doing it unless you had coppied it from mine and I thought I had intrusted it in the hands of a person who had more regard to the dictates of Honor and Justice than to take the undue advantage you have done of the confidence and trust I imposed in you. But I find I was mistaken and after being at the great Trouble and Expence of making a design, paying for paper, printing &c find myself in the most ingenerous Manner deprived not only of any proposed Adventage but even of the expence I have been at as truly as if you had plundered me on the highway. If you are insensible of the Dishonour you have brought on yourself by this Act, the world will not be so. However I leave you to reflect upon and consider one of the most dishonourable Actions you could well be guilty of.

This is a pretty strong accusation against a man with a clean record for probity and suggests that the basis may be a misunderstanding. We do not know Revere's response, for he has made no reference to the letter anywhere. He made no claim to designing the plate, which, like many of his other plates, bears the line *Engrav'd Printed & Sold by Paul Revere Boston*. We do know that Henry Pelham went ahead engraving his sketch, and on April 2, 1770, he inserted a notice in the *Boston Evening Post* and the *Boston Gazette* offering "an original print representing the late horrid massacre in King Street, taken on the spot." In the margin above it are three lines beginning: *The Fruits of Arbitrary Power, or the bloody massacre perpetrated in King Street,* then giving the names of the five killed and adding that six others were wounded, two of them fatally. Under the sketch is a quotation from the Psalms. When the Museum of Graphic Art of New York assembled its exhibit, American Printmaking: the First 150 Years, it exhibited Pelham's print as the prototype of engraving of the Boston Massacre. Only two prints are known, one in the New York Public Library and one in the American Antiquarian Society. As for Pelham's angry outburst, Miss Esther Forbes discovered that a year or so later Pelham and Revere seemed to have made a satisfactory business arrangement, for Revere was handling Pelham's print.

One other puzzle is associated with the massacre. Who drew the pen-and-ink outline of the buildings on King Street, showing the spots where the victims fell, which was used at the trial of the soldiers? It was owned at one time by Mellen Chamberlain, a former librarian of the Boston Public Library, who, in a book published in 1887, identified it as having been made by Revere and used at the trial. Miss Forbes scrutinized the handwriting on it and concluded that this agreed with that of Revere's ledgers. But other doubts arise. Two of the victims in the sketch were evidently taken from the engraving. Revere may have lifted them; on the other hand Pelham, who asserted his print was "taken on the spot," may have drawn them. So the puzzle remains.

There were now two identical prints of the Boston massacre on the market and Revere's was by far the most popular. As propaganda it must have had immense influence on the other American colonies, who were as unfriendly to British soldiers as the Bostonians. Revere engraved many other colonial scenes, some strictly propaganda against the British. One of his most admired prints shows the British ships of war landing British troops on Long Wharf at Boston in 1768, which he published three weeks after his massacre print. The design and coloring are credited to Christian Remick, who drew a number of sketches for Revere. Another engraving of the massacre, taken from Revere, was made by Jonathan Mulliken of Newburyport. Miss Wendy J. Shadwell, curator of the great Middendorf collection of prints, in the catalogue of the exhibit writes that Revere, appropriator of Pelham's design, was in turn the victim of a borrower. Mulliken changed only a few details of Revere's engraving. The presumption is that he also published it in 1770, and in Newburyport, where he was a clock- and watchmaker.

A third copy was published in the *Freeholders Magazine or Monthly Chronicle of Liberty* of London, proving that the opposition could express itself freely there. It was based on the Pelham print and had been altered by removal of the moon, the clock, and the unperturbed dog.

When Pelham drew his sketch he was obviously as bitter as any of the Sons of Liberty, but his subsequent temper was quite different. He was a half-brother of John Singleton Copley, who was about ten years his senior. When that extraordinary painter, who was entirely self-educated, sent his first portrait to Benjamin West in London, it was *The Boy and the Flying Squirrel,* in which Harry (Henry) Pelham was the boy. West recognized the originality of the painter and had his work put on exhibition at the Royal Academy, disregarding some stringent rules that would have kept it out. Copley, who was Boston born, was less than a year old when his father died, and about nine when his mother married a painter and engraver named Peter Pelham, who had a reputation as a portraitist. Peter Pelham died in 1751, and Mary Copley opened a tobacco shop in Bowdoin Square to support her family. It is ironic that Henry Pelham, who designed the biggest piece of anti-British propaganda, remained in Boston during the siege, and when Major General William Howe evacuated the town and provided passage on ships for Tories, Pelham went with them and never returned to America.

2

The Purloined Letters

❧

IN THE SPRING of 1773 the patriots of the Massachusetts Assembly unexpectedly received incontrovertible proof that
Governor Hutchinson and several other Crown officials
had been advising members of Parliament to curtail the
liberties of the colonists and adopt measures for tighter
controls from the top. This information came in a packet
of letters that had been placed in the hands of Benjamin
Franklin by an unidentified source in London and sent by
him to Thomas Cushing, Speaker of the House, to be
shown confidentially to a small number of his liberal associates. Franklin said he had promised that the letters should
not be printed, nor should copies be made in whole or in
part, and they were to be returned. He explained that the
letters had been given him to prove that many of the measures that had made the Americans critical of Parliament
actually had been suggested by officials in Boston.

There were six letters by Hutchinson, written during
1768–1769, when he was Lieutenant Governor; four by

Andrew Oliver, Hutchinson's brother-in-law, who was Secretary of the Province; others by Charles Paxton and a few minor officials. They had been written to Thomas Whately, who had been Secretary of the Treasury Board under George Grenville, Secretary of the Exchequer at the time when the Treasury was devising new ways of squeezing revenue out of the colonies. Whately had died in June, 1772, and his brother William had become custodian of his papers.

In 1770 Franklin had been asked by the Massachusetts Assembly to act as Agent for the Province in London. He was already acting in a similar capacity for Pennsylvania, Georgia, and New Jersey, and had successfully interpreted the opposition of the colonies to the Stamp Act. When he presented his Massachusetts credentials to Lord Hillsborough, who had charge of American affairs in the ministry of Lord North, he was rudely told that a commission from the Massachusetts Assembly was invalid without the consent of the Governor, and this Hutchinson had refused to give. Franklin, who had great contempt for Hillsborough's methods, considering his conduct of American affairs perverse and senseless, told Hillsborough he could not conceive why the consent of the Governor should be thought necessary to the appointment of an agent for the people. "It is the business of the people that is to be done," said Franklin; "he is not one of them. He is himself an agent."

"Whose agent is he?" asked Hillsborough.

"The King's, my Lord."

"No such matter . . . No agent can be appointed but by an act, nor any act pass without his assent. Besides, this proceeding is directly contrary to express instructions."

Franklin had never heard of any instructions and went calmly on his way, presenting the views of the Assembly and trying to bridge the gap of understanding between Parliament and the colonies.

The contents of the letters did not vary greatly from the known views of the Tory writers, but their offense lay in that they were written to influence legislation against the popular cause. Hutchinson, a native son, stressed his love for New England, as always, but he evidently wanted a country where the plain people took orders from a few privileged persons appointed by the Crown. His perennial insecurity also came out in his writings; he was fearful of a possible breach of relations with England and doubted that the colonies could navigate alone. He had written: "I never think of the measures necessary for the peace and good order of the colonies without pain . . . I doubt whether it is possible to project a system of government in which a colony 3,000 miles distant from the parent state shall enjoy all the liberty of the parent state. There must be an abridgment of what are called English liberties. I wish the good of the colony when I wish to see some further restraint of liberty, rather than [that] the connection with the parent state should be broken, for I am sure such a break must prove the ruin of the colony."

Hutchinson had sharp epithets for the liberals. Their leaders were incendiaries—his favorite term; he had called Samuel Adams "the great incendiary." The Sons of Liberty were engaged in licentiousness; the newspapers were scandalous. He abhorred the levelling nature of the town meeting, in which the citizens spoke their minds: "Ignorant though they be, yet the heads of Boston town meeting influence all public measures." He had told

Lord Hillsborough that the Tories of Boston "decline attending town meetings where they are sure of being out-voted by men of the lowest order, all being admitted."

Oliver expressed similar distrust of popular government and suggested changes that would keep control well in the hands of the aristocrats. He wanted the colonies represented in Parliament, but his views gave no support to a popular choice for representative. He wanted the Council composed entirely of landed proprietors, and a further tightening of administration by abolishing the popular election of grand juries. He was not the only American-born official who believed the people could not be trusted to dispense justice.

Speaker Cushing thought it would be difficult to make use of the letters. Samuel Adams and John Adams were enraged by them. Samuel had protested, when a collection of official letters was being sent to London on a previous occasion, that all such correspondence about the Province should be public. John Adams read the letters while riding the judicial circuit and sharply expressed his indignation. "These curious projectors and speculators in politics will ruin this country," he commented. "The secrecy of these epistolary genii is very remarkable; profoundly secret, dark and deep." He could hardly find words strong enough to characterize Hutchinson. "Cool, thinking, deliberate villain, malicious and vindictive, as well as ambitious and avaricious . . . Bone of our bone, born and educated among us! Mr. Hancock is deeply affected, is determined with Major Hawley to watch this vile serpent and his deputy, Brattle."

Once the letters had been read by the leaders, it became difficult to keep secret what they contained. The letters had arrived in March; in June the House was convened in executive session and Samuel Adams, as clerk, read the letters to the members. Their resentment was intense. By a vote of 106, with only five dissenting, they adopted resolutions censuring the officials for sowing discord and attempting to subvert the constitution by introducing arbitrary power. They asked the King to remove both Hutchinson and Oliver from office.

The leaders now tried to evade Franklin's condition that the letters be not copied or printed. They asked Governor Hutchinson whether he had written them and would give them copies. He replied: "If you desire copies with a view to make them public, the originals are more proper for the purpose than the copies." This was construed as overcoming the restriction, and the letters were printed and distributed to the other colonies.

Weeks later word of the disclosures in Boston reached London. The furore that followed was caused less by the exposure of the views of the royal officials than by the enormity of violating the private correspondence of Englishmen. Yet British officials had no scruples about opening letters that passed through the postal service, and Benjamin Franklin himself had discovered that some of his correspondence from America had been opened and badly resealed. Since no one knew how the letters had reached America suspicions raised old animosities. The letters had been written to Thomas Whately, who had been Secretary of the Treasury Board under George Grenville, Secretary of the Exchequer at the time when the Treasury was devising new ways of squeezing revenue out of the colonies. Whately had died in June, 1772, and his brother William had become executor of the estate. William denied

that he had removed any of his brother's letters, but recalled that John Temple, who had been Surveyor of Customs for the Northern District, had consulted his own
letters in the files. In the charges made in newspapers by
Whately Temple considered himself libelled and challenged him to a duel, in which Whately was seriously
wounded.

Franklin had kept mum while London was arguing over
the letters, but when he learned that the Temple-Whately
duel was likely to be resumed when Whately mended he
determined to speak out. He published a letter in the *Public Advertiser* asserting that it was he who had sent the
incriminating letters to Boston. He did not say how he had
obtained them, but asserted neither Whately nor Temple
had access to them. Temple, who later became a baronet,
privately contradicted Franklin. Franklin offered no apology but pleaded that as Agent for Massachusetts it was his
duty to inform the Province, since the letters were written
"by public officers to persons in public stations, on public
affairs, and intended to produce public measures."

The Tories were openly contemptuous and even Franklin's Whig friends found it difficult to excuse what they
considered conduct unbecoming a gentleman.

The Massachusetts Assembly had sent its petition asking for the removal from office of Hutchinson and Oliver
to Franklin, for submission to the King. Lord Dartmouth,
now Secretary of State for the Colonies, took on the mis-
sion in August. In December the King sent the petition to
the Privy Council for a formal hearing. In January Franklin
was informed that the Lords' Committee of the Privy
Council on Plantation Affairs would consider the petition,
and told to be present. In a first meeting at the Cockpit it

became clear that the Solicitor General, Alexander Wedderburn, who was known for his abusive methods in court, was going to interrogate Franklin about the letters. Franklin asked for counsel and was given three weeks to prepare his case.

When the Committee met again late in February all the privy councillors were present, as well as numerous lords who were aching to see Franklin humiliated. Some men who thought well of Franklin were present too, among them Edmund Burke, Jeremy Bentham, and Joseph Priestley, but there were many others who detested Franklin, such as Lord Hillsborough. John Dunning and John Lee, counsel for Franklin, ably presented the case for the petition which asked the removal of Hutchinson and Oliver, but Wedderburn ridiculed the charges and asserted that the officials had been able public servants, and that London, and not Hutchinson, had ordered troops to Boston. Wedderburn, called by Carl van Doren "the government's master of abuse," then began to denounce Franklin in the most violent terms as a common thief. W. E. H. Lecky, in his *History of England in the Eighteenth Century* quotes him as saying:

"How the letters came into the possession of anyone but the rightful owners is still a mystery for Dr. Franklin to explain. He was not the rightful owner, and they could not have come into his hands by fair means. Nothing will acquit Dr. Franklin of the charge of obtaining them by fraudulent or corrupt means for the most malignant of purposes, unless he stole them from the person who stole them. I hope, my Lords, you will brand this man for the honor of this country, of Europe, and of mankind. Into what country will the fabricator of this iniquity hereafter go with unembarrassed face? Men will watch him with a jealous eye . . . It is impossible to read his account, expressive of the coolest and most deliberate malice, without horror."

Lecky appreciated the dramatic character of Franklin's confrontation, declaring that it was well suited to the brush of an historical painter. Lecky saw Franklin as an old man of sixtyseven, "the greatest writer, the greatest philosopher America had produced, a member of some of the chief scientific societies in Europe, the accredited representative of the most important of the colonies of America, and for nearly an hour and in the midst of the most distinguished of living Englishmen he was compelled to hear himself denounced as a thief or the accomplice of thieves. He stood there conspicuous and erect, and without moving a muscle amid the torrent of invective, but his apparent composure was shared by few who were about him. With the single exception of Lord North, the Privy Councillors who were present lost all dignity and all self-respect."

The Committee of the Privy Council lost no time in rejecting the petition of Massachusetts to remove Hutchinson and Oliver from office, calling it "false, groundless and scandalous, and calculated only for the seditious purpose of keeping up a spirit of clamor and discontent in the Province." With the approval of the King Franklin was dismissed from the office of Deputy Postmaster General for the Colonies—"ignominiously," says Lecky. The historian adds: "It was an office which had yielded no revenue before he had received it, but which his admirable organization had made lucrative and important."

3

Dissent Becomes Violent

✿

NOTHING in pre-Revolutionary history exceeds the exuberance with which the people of Boston and environs welcomed and cheered the Boston Tea Party. Here the patriots planned and carried out the destruction of a large quantity of private property, owned by a corporation that had not precipitated the dispute. Up to this time all demonstrations against British tax policies arranged by the liberal leaders had been orderly and, as Samuel Adams insisted, legal, and although mobs had become unruly on several occasions, their actions had been unforeseen. The Boston Tea Party, however, had been planned in great detail; it was carried out by some of the best-known men of the town, who had carefully disguised themselves and awaited a signal to engage in large-scale destruction. It is true that several days were taken up trying to get a peaceful withdrawal of the tea ships from Boston Harbor, and that such efforts failed, but from all accounts the town was tense and excited all this time. Two Town Meetings were packed with people eager for a showdown, the cadets of the Boston militia regiment were exercising with vigor on the Common, and hundreds of sympathizers were arriving from all parts of the Province and swelling the crowds.

The Boston Tea Party of December 16, 1773, marks the peak of the resistance of the Massachusetts patriots to the taxation policies of Great Britain. It is the culmination of the campaign of opposition that had been accelerating for twenty years and included the vain fight against the Writs of Assistance and the partly successful efforts to frustrate operation of the Stamp Act and the Townshend Acts. These two measures had been repealed, but the tax on tea remained, and the injury to the principles of the colonists was compounded in the spring of 1773, when Parliament passed a new modified Tea Act. By this time the Americans of the Atlantic Seaboard were cooperating better than formerly in uniting their methods of opposition, and Samuel Adams, using the Committees of Correspondence that he had originated, was able to get support for his programs in Pennsylvania, Virginia, South Carolina, and to some extent in New York.

The Tea Act of 1773 was presented to Parliament by the King's First Minister, Lord North, who had become Chancellor of the Exchequer when Townshend died in 1769, and succeeded the Duke of Grafton in January, 1770. It was Lord North who had presented the repeal of the Townshend Acts—except that on tea—to the House of Commons on March 5, 1770, on the evening of which the Boston Massacre exploded in Boston. Tea was an important commodity in the British economy and even affected the country's foreign policies, for the East India Company had developed extensive holdings in India, which had to be protected by British arms. The nonimportation agreements by American merchants had cut its shipments to the colonies to an unprofitable quantity; the colonists now either abstained entirely from drinking tea or obtained tea smuggled in from Dutch ports. New York and Pennsylvania were the chief beneficiaries of smuggling; Boston tried to brew "Labrador tea," made from an herb, but too bitter to become popular.

The leaders had been most successful in inducing Boston not to use tea; a large assembly in Faneuil Hall had decided for total abstinence; 410 families were said to have abjured tea drinking and 120 young women calling themselves the Daughters of Liberty had given up "the drinking of foreign tea, in hope to frustrate a plan that tends to deprive a whole community of all that is valuable in life." John Adams learned how firm a Daughter could be when he asked a hostess: "Is it lawful for a weary traveler to refresh himself with a dish of tea, provided it has been honestly smuggled and paid no duties?" The lady replied: "We have renounced all tea in this place, but I'll make you coffee."

Tea was produced in such huge crops in the Orient that not all the tea drinking in England was sufficient to use up the supply without the help of addicts in America. In 1773 the East India Company had 17,000,000 pounds of tea in its English warehouses and attempted to get a subsidy from the government. The proposal was made that Britain remove the American tax of three pence, which would enable the East India Company to undersell all foreign tea on the American market. Parliament, however, passed an act removing the export duty that had been paid by the company and retained the tax on tea sold to the colonies. Thus the company could sell its tea cheaper, but the tax grievance remained. England had not capitulated to the colonies. It takes little imagination to see that a big crisis in the relations of the colonies with Great Britain could have been averted with the exercise of a little comprehension—and common sense—by the stiffnecked members of Parliament.

There were odious conditions attached to the act. Tea was to be handled in the colonies by consignees named by the company, thus ignoring the merchants who had taken part in the nonimportation campaign. The Boston people were further irritated when it became known that among the consignees were two sons and a nephew of Governor Hutchinson. As word reached Boston that ships laden with tea were on their way preparations were made for their reception. The patriotic committees in American ports organized public protests. The first act in Boston was to call upon all the consignees to resign their offices publicly under the Liberty Tree; this they declined to do, but eventually they offered their resignations to the Governor and Council, who refused to receive them. In fear that they might suffer physical injury—the Sons had a way with tar and feathers, and the windows of Richard Clarke's house already had been broken—they moved for protection to Castle William.

The first of the tea ships, the *Dartmouth*, with 114 chests of tea, arrived on November 28. The Boston committee was alert; it posted a broadside saying "That worst of plagues, the detested tea, shipped for this port by the East India Company, is now arrived in the harbor; the hour of destruction, or manly opposition to the machinations of tyranny stares you in the face; every friend to his country, to himself and to posterity, is now called upon to meet at Faneuil Hall at 9 o'clock this day (Monday, November 29) at which time the bells will ring, to make united and successful resistance to this worst, and most destructive measure of administration." The strident notes of this call show how far the leaders had moved since the Boston Massacre from calm and carefully considered attempts to negotiate. The antagonism was now open; the repeated harshness of Parliament, and the unfriendly disdain of the administration, had brought the patriots, who completely dominated the Province, to open hostility. At the Monday meeting the town voted to permit no payment of duty nor landing of tea. The ship was ordered to Griffin's wharf and a guard of twentyfive men placed on her. The consignees asked that the tea be stored while they wrote to England for instructions; the townsmen refused the request. The sheriff read a communication from the Governor, ordering the meeting to disperse; this was hissed down. The Committee of Safety of the Sons of Liberty sent six men riding forth to alert other communities; one of the men was Paul Revere.

Two other ships, the *Beaver* and the *Eleanor*, carrying 228 chests of tea, arrived before December 14 and moored at Griffin's wharf. On that day another huge town meeting was held in Old South Meeting House. The leaders urged the owner of the *Dartmouth*, named Rotch, to turn about and sail back to England, but he said he would endanger ship and cargo unless he had a clearance from the customs, which the commissioner refused to give because the duty had not been paid. The leaders then decided to send Rotch with a committee to Governor Hutchinson to get an order from him. Hutchinson had gone to his country house in Milton, and when Rotch arrived there with his request, the Governor said that "consistent to the rules of government and his duty to the King he could not grant one without they produced a previous clearance from the [customs] office." It took all afternoon and until dusk for Rotch to make the round trip, and when he reached the assembly in Old South, which had been listening to fervent patriotic oratory by Josiah Quincy, Jr., the candles were already lighted. When Samuel Adams had reported the Governor's answer he announced: "This meeting can do nothing more to save the country."

This apparently was a signal for war whoops both inside and outside the hall; outside appeared a gang of men with blackened faces and made up like Indians, who called themselves Mohawks. With shouts and cheers the Mohawks led the way two-by-two to Griffin's wharf, followed by an immense crowd. There was nothing spontaneous about the proceeding, which had been carefully planned. The Mohawks boarded the three tea ships and tossed 342 chests of tea into the harbor, without interference from the Governor or the regiments of General Gage's army stationed in Boston.

Although those who took part in the Boston Tea Party were wellknown to many people, they kept up the pretence of anonymity. Even fortyfive years later John Adams answered an inquiry from the editor of the *Niles Weekly Register* by saying that at the time of the tea party he did not know, or want to know, the Mohawks, because there might be future indictments and he would be likely to defend. "You may depend on it, they were no ordinary Mohawks," he said. "The profound secrecy in which they

have held their names, and the total absence of plunder,
are proofs of the characters of the men. I believe they
would have tarred and feathered any one of their number
who should have been detected in pocketing a pound of
hyson."

There was one eminent American who did not believe
dissent should be expressed by the destruction of private
property. He was Benjamin Franklin, then Agent for Massachusetts and resident in London. His reasonable letter
protesting the methods employed is rarely mentioned in
accounts of the "glorious day," but it deserves reprinting:

> To Thomas Cushing, Samuel Adams, John Hancock,
> William Phillips, of a Committee:
> I received the honor of your letter dated December 21
> containing a distinct account of the proceeding at Boston
> relative to the tea imported there, and of the circum-
> stances that occasioned its destruction. I communicated
> the same to Lord Dartmouth . . . It is unknown what
> other measures will be taken here on the occasion, but
> the clamor against the proceedings is high and general. I
> am truly concerned, as I believe all considerate men are
> with you, that there should seem to any a necessity for
> carrying matters to such an extremity as, in a dispute over
> political rights, to destroy private property; this (notwith-
> standing the blame justly due to those who obstructed the
> return of the tea) it is impossible to justify with people so
> prejudiced in favor of the power of Parliament to tax
> America, as most are in this country. As the India Com-
> pany, however, are not our adversaries, and the offensive
> measure of sending the tax did not take its rise with them,
> but was an expedient of the ministry to serve them and
> yet avoid a repeal of the old act, I cannot but wish and
> hope that before any compulsive measures are thought of
> here, our General Court will have shown a disposition to
> repair the damage and make compensation to the com-

pany. This all our friends here wish with me, and that if war is finally to be made upon us, which some threaten, an act of violent injustice on our part, unrectified, may now give a colorable pretence for it. A speedy reparation will immediately set us right in the opinion of all Europe. And though the mischief was the act of persons unknown, yet as probably they cannot be found or brought to answer for it, there seem to be some reasonable claims on the society at large in which it happened. Making voluntarily such reparation can be no dishonor to us or prejudice to our claim of rights, since Parliament here has frequently considered in the same light similar cases, and only a few years since, when a valuable sawmill, which had been erected at great expense, was violently destroyed by a number of persons suspected to be sawyers, but unknown, a grant was made out of the public treasury of 2,000 pounds to the owner as compensation. I hope in thus freely (and perhaps too forwardly expressing my sentiments and wishes,) I shall not give offense to any. I am sure I mean well, being ever with sincere affection to my native country and great respect to the Assembly and yourselves.

Gentlemen, your most obedient and humble servant,

B. Franklin

One result of the Boston Tea Party was the Port Act, which closed the Port of Boston and stopped all commerce. The British government took up the charter of Massachusetts, quartered troops in Boston, and ordered all offenders to be tried in Nova Scotia or England. In the resultant outburst of rage all opportunity for reconciliation with England was gone. Through his Committees of Correspondence Samuel Adams now built up resistance in the colonies and Virginia called for the first Continental Congress, which met in Philadelphia September 5 to October 26, 1774.

4

Other Tactics of Protest

FOR YEARS the American spokesmen for liberty and natural rights countered every attempt of Parliament to impose a tax for revenue on the colonies with the declaration that such a tax was illegal because the colonies had no share in making it. Every schoolboy who has read American history knows that *Taxation Without Representation* was the great slogan in political warfare, one of the primary grievances that led to the American Revolution.

Samuel Adams asserted this repeatedly; Benjamin Franklin brought it to the attention of Members of Parliament; James Otis summarized the protest in the ringing declaration: *Taxation without representation is tyranny.* Otis lost no opportunity to condemn arbitrary acts that deprived a man of his property without justification or consent. In 1764 he said; "Taxes must not be laid on the people but by their consent in person or by deputation." The repetition of these and similar statements by the popular faction in Massachusetts must have become known to all officials of the British Government.

The question then arises: Did the American leaders ever initiate action to get representation in Parliament?

They did not. Actually, they did not want representation. They wanted to levy their own taxes and would have been embarrassed if Parliament had voted to seat their representatives. Samuel Adams must have become apprehensive when he learned that Governor Bernard had recommended to the British Government that the colonies be given representation in the House of Commons. Before the relations between the Massachusetts House and the administration became estranged Bernard had expressed his interest in reforms that would benefit the Province. In October, 1765, when the town of Boston was arguing with Bernard over stamp duties, it told him that according to the charter the right of representation was in the same body that exercised the power of taxation, but that Massachusetts was not represented in Parliament, "and indeed we think it impracticable." This must have been a great surprise to Bernard, who may have thought the liberals really wanted representation.

Some time in 1765 Samuel Adams must have had a big scare. He could have had the horrible thought: Suppose Parliament grants representation? He and the rest of the patriots had made such an issue of nonrepresentation there was reason to believe that one of the friends of America in the House of Commons might agitate toward it. Adams made a quick disclaimer. He did not want representation at any price. He had to caution the other assemblies not to make this mistake. In the same month that he had informed Governor Bernard, the Massachusetts House on October 29, 1765, voted fourteen resolutions on all the issues on which it took a stand, and the fourteenth read thus:

"Resolved, that the inhabitants of this Province are not and never can be represented in the Parliament of Great Britain, and that such a representation there as the subjects of Great Britain do actually and rightfully enjoy is impracticable for the subjects in America. And further, that in the opinion of this House the several subordinate powers of legislation in America were constituted upon the apprehensions of this impracticability."

By 1768 the possibility of getting representation in Parliament must still have been an issue, for the liberals were wary. In January the House authorized an instruction to Denys DeBerdt, Agent for Massachusetts in London, also prepared by Adams:

"You will observe that the House still insists upon that inestimable right of being taxed only by representatives of their own free election, which they think is infringed by the late acts for establishing a revenue in America. It is by no means to be understood that they desire a representation in Parliament, because, by reason of local circumstances, it is impracticable that they should be equally and fairly represented. There is nothing therefore, which I apprehend the colonies would more dread."

The House now decided that an attempt should be made to harmonize the points of view of the various houses of representatives and burgesses on the continent. On February 11 it appointed a committee composed of Samuel Adams, Otis, Cushing, Bowers, Hawley, Dexter, and Richmond to prepare a letter to the other provinces, explaining why there should be no representation in Parliament. After declaring that all the colonies maintained their full rights under the British Constitution, the letter said they "cannot be represented in Parliament, and that it will forever be impracticable that they should be equally represented there, and consequently not at all, being separated by an ocean of a thousand leagues, and that his majesty's royal predecessors for this reason were graciously pleased to form a subordinate legislature here, that their subjects might enjoy the inalienable right of representation. Also, conceding the utter improbability of their even being fully and equally represented in Parliament, and the great expense that must inavoidably attend even a partial representation there . . ."

That was certainly an effective warning, for when it came to expense the members of the assemblies were extremely careful about costs.

In January, 1775, when the patriots were busy storing up muskets, Daniel Leonard, a Tory who signed himself Massachusettensis appealed in the *Boston Post Boy:* "Why not try for representation?" John Adams quickly turned him aside. He explained the colonies would not have sufficient members in Parliament to give them a controlling voice in their affairs.

Finally, there was the flat statement to General Henry S. Conway, America's friend in the House of Commons, on February 13, 1768: "The people of this Province would by no means be inclined to petition the Parliament for a representation."

It is clear then that the slogan of *taxation without representation*, which gained such tremendous currency in the thirteen colonies before the Revolution, was intended to give Parliament a good reason for not taxing them. What would have happened if Parliament had suddenly reversed itself and accepted the colonies as components of the empire is one of those "ifs" of history that can be discussed today without heat or consequences.

5

The Commemorative Orations

NOBODY IN THE colonies was allowed to forget the Boston
Massacre. To the patriots it was Exhibit A in their argument against standing armies. They used it unsparingly to
prove the arrogance of the British command in America.
No doubt it spurred the collecting and secreting of weapons and ammunition in towns and crossroads hamlets. In a
more formal manner it was commemorated on March 5 in
thirteen subsequent years by orations, which continued
until celebrations of Independence Day became more important.

James Lovell, later active in framing the Articles of
Confederation, gave the first oration in 1771 in the Old
South Meeting House. He was followed by Dr. Joseph
Warren, Dr. Benjamin Church, and John Hancock. When
March, 1775, came around the patriots were drilling and
piling up arms and General Gage was calling the Provincial
Congress an unlawful assembly that was drawing the in-
habitants toward "perjuries, riots, sedition, treason, and

rebellion." John Hancock, president of the Congress, was asking that "such persons as are skilled in the manufacturing of firearms and bayonets be encouraged diligently to apply themselves thereto for supplying such of the inhabitants as shall be deficient." Despite this growing hostility Dr. Joseph Warren determined to give a massacre oration, for the second time, and to extol patriotic idealism in a beleaguered city, where the British Army now had eleven regiments of infantry and four companies of artillery. Because March 5 fell on a Sunday the address was set for Monday, and because town meetings were banned by the military, the patriots announced an adjourned session of the Port Bill meeting of the previous June.

When the time came the church was packed with people, a large proportion of them British soldiers. When their officers arrived Samuel Adams asked the people in the front pews to make place for them. When Warren could not make his way inside he crawled through a window to reach the pulpit. Soldiers sat at both sides of him, but his speech was forthright and uncompromising. He demanded to know whether the ruin that faced Boston had come from "some fiend, fresh from the depths of hell," and answered: "No, it is the hand of Britain that inflicts the wound. The arms of George, our rightful King, have been employed to shed that blood which freely should have flowed at his command, when justice or the honor of his crown had called his subjects to the field." One officer, imitating an Indian gesture when the choice was peace or war, held up some bullets in his palm; Warren dropped his handkerchief over them and went on unperturbed.

John Adams and some of his associates had been surprised when Samuel Adams and Samuel Pemberton, acting for a standing committee of the town of Boston, invited John to give the oration on March 5, 1772. Samuel had put in many months denouncing the outcome of the massacre trials and insisting on the guilt of the military, which John had defended so successfully. The committee was well aware of John Adams' aversion to speaking, but they persisted. John began to make excuses, blaming his "feeble state of health." He was in one of his uncooperative moods and said he wanted to avoid even thinking about public affairs. Moreover, he was "too old to make declamations" —at 36! He was "clearly, fully, absolutely, and unalterably determined against it."

Actually, he was still smarting under public criticism of his conduct two years before, although his fellow townsmen had given proof of their respect for him by electing him to a seat in the Assembly. He explained this when he had time to write in his diary. "I thought the reason that had hitherto actuated the town was enough, namely, the part I took in the trial of the soldiers. Though the subject of the oration was quite compatible with the verdict of the jury in that case, and indeed even with the absolute innocence of the soldiers, yet I found the world in general were not capable or not willing to make the distinction, and therefore, by making an oration on this occasion, I should only expose myself to the lash of ignorant and malicious tongues on both sides of the question."

The committeemen asked John to keep their invitation a secret, probably to avoid hurting the feelings of an alternative choice, and bore John no ill will. The next day John went to Samuel's house and was so well received that he felt a twinge of regret. The place had just been newly papered and decorated, and was "a very genteel house."

Moreover, Samuel "was more cool, genteel, and agreeable than common; concealed and restrained his passions." John was sorry he had been intemperate.

At the third anniversary, in 1773, Dr. Benjamin Church gave the oration and John attended. Church was still associating with the patriots, and apparently had not yet gone over to the Tories. He was unmasked some time later through a personal letter delivered at a wrong address. His defection was a rude shock, because he had been close to the leaders in Boston, and his end was tragic, for he was lost at sea. John Adams approved his discourse, and it prompted him to reassure himself that defending the British soldiers was one of "the most gallant, generous, manly and disinterested actions of my whole life, and one of the best pieces of service I ever rendered my own country. Judgment of death against those soldiers would have been as foul a stain upon this country as the executions of the Quakers or witches anciently. This, however, is no reason why the town should not call the action of that night a massacre; nor is it any argument in favor of the Governor or minister who caused them to be sent here. But it is the strongest of proofs of the danger of standing armies."

The commemorative oration had a vital place in the affairs of Boston, even if the speaker brought no new illumination to the subject of the massacre. John Adams recorded the pleasure he and his intimates felt when John Hancock surpassed himself in eloquence at the exercises of March 5, 1774. Adams found Hancock's oration "an elegant, a pathetic, a spirited performance," using pathetic in its favorable sense. He saw "a vast crowd, rainy eyes." Men and women wept easily in the eighteenth century.

Adams praised Hancock's composition, pronunciation, and action, but his real praise was for Hancock's condemnation of pride in riches, which had no relation to the issues raised by the massacre and was rather a sermon. At that time sermons obviously answered a need for admonition, judging by the frequency with which they were quoted. "With singular dignity and grace," Hancock, a rich man, possibly the richest in Massachusetts, condemned avarice. He said: "Despise the glare of wealth. The people who pay greater respect to a wealthy villain, than to an honest, upright man in poverty, almost deserve to be enslaved; they plainly show that wealth, however it may be acquired, is in their esteem to be preferred to virtue."

But the word went around Boston that Hancock's oration actually was written for him by Dr. Samuel Cooper, who thus seized the occasion to have a rich man condemn avarice.

The Warren oration of 1775 preceded by only a few weeks the battles of Lexington and Concord, and the defense of Bunker Hill, in which Warren died. The 1776 oration was delivered by the Reverend Peter Thacher in Watertown, and subsequent orations were given elsewhere until the siege of Boston was lifted. They ceased in 1783, when Independence Day became a greater occasion for patriotic oratory.

The Town House of 200 years ago, around which the events of this chronicle occurred, has passed through many mutations since 1770, but restoration and care probably have made it more attractive today than it was in colonial times. It is now known as the Old State House, for after the British departed the government of the Commonwealth of Massachusetts used it. The first Town House had been erected in 1658 and for fifty years had sheltered a succession of royal governors, judges and town officials. In 1711 it burned down, and in 1713 the government opened a new Town House, built of brick. It suffered from a severe fire in 1747, but the walls remained firm and it was in the restored building that Governor and Council met. It faced King Street, now State, which led down to Dock Square. At the corner of King Street and Royal Exchange Lane stood the Custom House, where the affair of 1770 began.

When Charles Bulfinch completed the new State House with the gilded dome on Beacon Hill in 1795, the government turned the old State House over to the city of Boston, which used it until a new City Hall was built in School Street in 1865. Thereafter no one seemed to have any interest in the old structure. M. A. DeWolfe Howe wrote in *Boston Landmarks* that now it "touched its all-time low. Disfigured by a mansard roof and plastered with signs of the inward uses of the building, for brokerage, insurance, telegraph, railroad, and steamship offices, it appears in a contemporary drawing as a mess of the first order."

Apparently the old building aroused no sentimental feelings during the celebration of the centennial anniversaries in the 1870's. When Boston learned that the land on which it stood was worth $1,500,000 it voted, in 1881, to tear it down. Fortunately there were patriots in Chicago who already had one authentic memorial of the American Revolution in the grave of David Kinnison, veteran of the Boston Tea Party, who had died in 1851, aged 115, and was buried in Lincoln Park. Chicago offered to buy the Old State House and transport it brick by brick to Chicago. This was too crass for members of patriotic and historical societies in Boston. They determined that the Old State House must be preserved. The city fathers agreed to stand the loss on the land in perpetuity, and never again to threaten the building with removal or destruction. The work of restoration began. The offending signs and the mansard roof were removed; the original layouts were followed for council chamber, staircases, window frames and balcony. In 1882 it was rededicated. In the midst of Boston's tall buildings it stands as a little gem in the classical tradition, with a graceful tower topped by a cupola, stepped gables reminiscent of Dutch houses, and two ornaments that once were regarded with scorn and today are prized as antiques—the British lion and the unicorn, rampant, as their predecessors appeared on the night of March 5, 1770. And in State Street near the Old State House is a circle that marks the spot where the victims of the Boston Massacre fell.

Another government building of 1770 was the Province House, located on Washington Street at the head of Milk Street. Although it was used for official business by the royal governors and by General Thomas Gage, it inspired no historical interest. It was three stories tall, decorated with the arms of Britain, and surmounted by a large cupola. By the middle of the nineteenth century it was completely surrounded by tall structures, and after much misuse it was pulled down.

Boston and Philadelphia are the two American cities where the glorious events of the American Revolution were commemorated longer and more intensively than anywhere else. Men who had fought at Bemis Heights and frozen their feet at Valley Forge were still alive in the early decades of the nineteenth century, and a great many who had reached maturity in the days of Daniel Webster and John Quincy Adams had heard fathers and grand-fathers repeat tales of the campaigns. Families bore names that had been on the rosters of the first settlements, and it was not until mid-century that the voting lists of Boston began to include many Irishmen. With them came a revival of the hatred for Great Britain, for the British had throt-tled Irish trade in the same manner that they had tried to restrict the colonies. This gave new zest to the parades and orations on Independence Day, and the older Bostonians, such as the Ancient and Honorable Artillery, joined cheerfully with the marching Hibernians.

The Boston Massacre found a sympathetic response in northern Ireland. Belfast whigs informed the *Freeman's Journal* that the 29th Regiment of Foot had a profligate record when quartered in Belfast. The Irish were quick to suspect that the British Government intended to increase its military commitments in America in order to enforce its revenue laws. Radicals in Ireland shared the fears of Pur-itan New England that the Church of England would establish an episcopate in the colonies. The perennial land troubles in Ireland already were turning the eyes of its young men to the western world, and one report said that 37,000 Irish people emigrated to America in five years, 1767–1774, just prior to the outbreak of the Revolution.

The historical societies remained strongly conservative

in their memberships, and occupied themselves with collecting and preserving records and memoirs of the great past. They refused to give mob action equal weight with heroism on the battlefield. When, in 1887, the General Court of Massachusetts voted to erect a monument to the victims of the Boston Massacre, the majority of the members of the Massachusetts Historical Society quickly expressed their disapproval. There was at that time no stone or other marker in the Old Granary Burying Ground to indicate where, as one dissenter said, the five had been left "wallowing in their gore." They were said to be lying near the Chetley tomb, in close proximity to their great contemporary, Samuel Adams. Members of the society spoke of them as "vulgar ruffians." Randolph G. Adams commented that the tide of historical interpretation indeed had turned. But it was like a weather vane. In 1900 the historian Samuel Abbott Green "veered back to the old interpretation of the event and indicated his disapproval of the Massachusetts Historical Society in 1887." The Boston Massacre, if not actually "the first battle of the Revolution," certainly remained an episode of enduring vitality.

Acknowledgments

THE BOSTON MASSACRE has a place in many memoirs, biographies, and histories dealing with the American Revolution. The transcript most easily available is the *Trial of the British Soldiers of the 29th Regiment of Foot*, of which the edition of 1824, published by William Emmons, is in the New York Public Library. Quite recently additions and variations have become available in the *Legal Papers of John Adams*, edited by L. Kinvin Wroth and Hiller B. Zobel, with L. H. Butterfield editing the documentation, issued by the Belknap Press of Harvard University Press and copyright, 1965, by the Massachusetts Historical Society. The editors published a summary of the trials, including new material, in the American Bar Association *Journal* for April, 1969. Before them Randolph G. Adams had found original material in the papers of the William L. Clements Library and first published it in the *Proceedings of the American Antiquarian Society* in 1937, including correspondence of General Thomas H.

Gage not available until then. It was entitled *New Light on the Boston Massacre*. Statements by Thomas Hutchinson that he had intended to make a part of his *History* were found by Mrs. Catherine Barton Mayo and published as *Additions to the History of the Province of Massachusetts Bay* in the *Proceedings of the American Antiquarian Society* in 1949. John Adams' account of the massacre is in his autobiography, included in the *Works of John Adams*, edited by his grandson, Charles Francis Adams, in 1856. The *Diary and Autobiography of John Adams*, edited by L. H. Butterfield and issued by the Belknap Press in 1961, is in many respects a more careful use of the materials. Most useful for reference have been articles in the *Proceedings of the Colonial Society of Massachusetts;* Frederick Kidder's *History of the Boston Massacre*, printed in the centennial year, 1870, which contains the *Trial* as well as the *Short Narrative of the Horrid Massacre in Boston*, and the *Observations*. O. M. Dickerson's thorough research for "Writs of Assistance as a Cause of the Revolution" appears in *The Era of the American Revolution*, a work commemorating the career of Evarts Boutell Greene, edited by Richard B. Morris, (Columbia University Press, 1939). Also valuable are Esther Forbes' *Paul Revere and the World He Lived In; American Criminal Trials*, by Peleg W. Chandler; the *Papers of Samuel Adams*, edited by L. H. Butterfield; Thomas Hutchinson's *History of the Province of Massachusetts Bay*; Carl van Doren's *Benjamin Franklin;* Stewart Beach's *Samuel Adams; The Fateful Years, 1764-76*, and *American Printmaking: The First 150 Years*.

Index